THE NEPALI FLAT

Gordon Alexander

www.gordonalexander.org

'Stop worrying about the potholes in the road and celebrate the journey.'

Fitzhugh Mullan

A special thanks to...

Clinton and Catherine Fearon for giving me permission to reproduce the lyrics of Clinton's song *Feelin' The Same*. *www*.clintonfearon.com

Lonely Planet, for the excellent guidance and allowing me to use their work. Reproduced with permission from Lonely Planet. © 2009 *Lonely Planet – Trekking in the Nepal Himalaya [9th Edition]*.

Hayloft Publishing, for allowing me to reproduce quotes from Ruth Hanson's excellent biography of Maurice Wilson: *A Yorkshireman on Everest*.

Tara Sola Y Cirera, Soham Gangopadhyay and openclipart.org for maps and illustrations.

Wikipedia, for all the facts and figures they make it so easy to come by.

Contents

Chapter One

ARRIVING IN KATHMANDU

They say that humans are made up of 60% water. Well for a Scotsman named Andy, who was sitting next to me on the flight from Kuala Lumpur to Kathmandu, that may be a little on the light side. About halfway through the flight, I looked over to see him, in the aisle seat with no one in between us, begin to flow (there is just no other word for it) in a downward motion towards the floor. I was reading *Lonely Planet: Trekking in the Nepal Himalaya*, but I closed the book and put it aside, for there was a far more interesting spectacle unfolding right next to me.

The flow was a little slow at first, but then accelerated after reaching the point of no return - a little above the hip region - and within seconds Andy's whole body was on the floor of the plane. The only thing preventing him from going further was the seat-belt, which was now secured around his neck.

I better do something, I thought.

I nudged him awake, and he looked around, utterly confused.

'Oh Jesus not again!' he cried out loud. 'I've got to stop falling asleep with my seatbelt on.'

'I think that's exactly what you're supposed to do,' I countered.

'Aye, but you won't end up choking yourself.'

His facts were irrefutable, so I opened my book once again, smiling as I heard his seatbelt un-click. Moments later I glanced over and realised that the human waterfall was in full flow once again. I gained some kind of guilty pleasure in watching this, like picking your nose at a set of traffic lights; because let us be fair, travelling is wonderful, but flying is about as boring as bat shit.

We were sitting in the first row of economy, with only a curtain separating us and business class. As the flow progressed, Andy's feet ended up in the front cabin, followed by his legs. He slipped entirely off the chair without even flinching, his lower body now in business class, with the rest of him in the aisle in economy. I let it go. He could no longer harm himself.

'Sir, sir! You can't do this!' hissed the air hostess once she realised what had happened. She scurried off towards the back of the plane, with Andy still out for the count, and came back with a glass of water. 'Wake up, wake up and drink!' she pleaded further.

'Oh not again!' Shouted Andy once again, this time loud enough to disturb people a few rows back. 'How long since I almost strangled myself?'

'That was literally about three minutes ago.'

'She's trying to give me water, look. She thinks because I'm Scottish I must be drunk.'

If it's any consolation to her, I thought that too.

*

This was my first time in Nepal. I had been planning to come here to trek in the Himalayas for almost a decade, but life sometimes gets in the way of living. The opportunity finally presented itself again and this time I seized it with both hands.

I arrived in Kathmandu on the last day of February, 2014. I arrived in a different world. We wandered like sheep through an old, tired-looking red brick building and it immediately became obvious who had been here before and who hadn't. The experienced few had printed off their visa documents, filled them out, had two passport photos ready and bee-lined for the two immigration officials waiting to process the entire flight.

I sensed a shit-fight, so I quickly filled out my visa application form, before fumbling in my bag for the passport photos that I thought I might need. *They must be in here somewhere*, I thought, although I was fast approaching the last possible hiding place.

'Do you want these in a little envelope so you don't lose them?' I remember my girlfriend at the time, Jo, asking me before I left.

'Nah, they'll be alright just flapping around loose in this book,' I'd said, or something ridiculously stupid like that. Well they were lost. Of course, she was right.

There was a little Nepali guy wandering around with an ancient camera, offering poor souls such as myself the opportunity to have their passport-sized photos taken. For $5 US, he could make it happen.

'I need photos, but I only have Australian dollars,' I said, immediately and naturally dumbing down my accent so that he could properly understand me.

'No problem, sah, just change money over there,' he said.

I wandered over to the only currency exchange place in the terminal and just kind of stood there and waited in front of an empty desk.

'We're closed!' boomed a voice from somewhere that I couldn't see. That was the end of that. I spied a solitary ATM a little way down. I skipped off towards it, but was dejected as I read the words 'OUT OF SERVICE' sticky-taped across the screen. I sighed and headed back to my little photographer mate.

'Sorry man, that place is closed and the ATM is out of service.'

'No problem, you got little money?'

'I only have fifty dollar notes,' I said while staring sheepishly at the floor.

The man looked at me with pity. He probably guessed this was the first time I had travelled anywhere. In my defence, I had not been to an airport without 24hr currency exchange and/or a working ATM; and when I'd asked the exchange man in Kuala Lumpur if he had Nepali money, he just laughed without even dignifying my enquiry with a response.

'No problem I fix,' he said while ushering me into his little photo booth. He snapped my tired-looking face. 'Get in queue.'

The queue was huge. Every single person on the plane was ahead of me and the line was not moving. I saw Andy ahead at the front and he was trying to get my attention. He was frantically waving at me to join him, but I made a gesture that said *I'm still waiting for my passport photos*, holding an imaginary camera up to my face and clicking the shutter button. He gave me a strange look and then turned back around. It was the half British part of me. I was just too good at queuing. All of a sudden the little camera man forcefully grabbed my arm and to my horror began to drag me to the immigration officer.

'You pay him visa,' he said.

'Australian dollars no problem?' I asked.

'No problem.'

The first mistake I'd made was to book the trip for 32 days instead of 30. The difference in visa price ended up being $100 US instead of $30. At that moment though, I really didn't give a shit. I gave the immigration officer $150 AU and he gave me change in American dollars. I gave the photographer $5, and then he reached into my hand and grabbed another $5 note and held it, still in my grasp, while making eye contact with me, as if asking for permission to take it. I nodded and he helped himself.

'You a very lucky mans,' he said. 'Many people in line and I get you straight to front.'

I thanked the man before stepping through to a second processing person, whose sole job, as far as I could tell, was to make sure his colleague before him had done his job, and to make the whole process half as efficient. I could feel 200 pairs of eyes boring into the back of my skull, but quite frankly I didn't really care. The whole process had taken well over an hour, even after leap-frogging everyone. But when I made my way through to baggage claim the bags still were not on the carrousel.

'Welcome to Kathmandu,' said Andy, who was leaning up against a pillar with a fed-up look on his face.

'It's not so bad, you just gotta bribe the photographer.'

The carrousel whirred to life. It sounded like an airplane was taking off inside the terminal building. As luck would have it, my bag was the second one out. I grabbed it and went to put it through the baggage scanner, but the customs official scolded me in a language I didn't understand. Disgust was oozing through his skin, and then he softened a little and waved me through. I sucked the part of my face between my lips and chin into my mouth while widening my eyes, as if to say, *what did I do to deserve that?*

I had arranged an airport pickup through the hotel as I wanted as little hassle as possible, and sure enough a big, burly looking Nepali man with a huge moustache was there, holding up a sign reading 'Mr. Alex'. *It must be me.*

'Hotel Friend's Home?' I asked him and he nodded and pointed towards his car. I jumped in and went to fasten my seatbelt, but I felt his hand on my arm, preventing me.

'No need seatbelt, sah,' he said. I think I had offended him.

'Ok, you must be good driver.'

'Yes,' was his only response.

It was after midnight now and very dark. Kathmandu lacked streetlights. We cruised past a gigantic looking showground with rides and fluorescent lights everywhere. *What the hell is going on?*

'This is Lord Shiva festival,' said the taxi man, as if reading my mind. 'Only day of the year that smoking the hashish is legal. Maybe you come one day too late.'

'Maybe,' I answered, shocked that his English was so good. He hooned around a group of stoned adolescents walking on the road, beeping his horn furiously. The roads were pretty empty, it was approaching 1am after all. But the drivers still found a way to make it chaotic. They beeped, throwing their headlights into high beam to alert oncoming traffic of their existence – the only real outcome, however, was to blind anyone coming the opposite way. He shot round a blind bend and successfully negotiated a pair of cows trotting down the middle of the road. Where the hell was I? I'd travelled Southeast Asia fairly extensively, as well as many places in the Middle East, but this

9

was just something else entirely. It was poorer, it was crazier. It was better! I was in love.

In the absence of traffic lights he turned in front of oncoming traffic and just expected them to stop or slow down. They did. I had jumped into the taxi a tired man, but now the adrenalin was pumping and I was thrilled.

He pulled into a narrow alley, barely wide enough for the taxi, and floored it down to a dead-end. He switched off the engine, turned to me and smiled. I looked out the window and read the sign, 'Hotel Friends Home'. Well we were here. I had no idea where here was, but we were there nonetheless. I paid the man the $10 US that the hotel advised me to pay while I was still in Australia, and was checked in by perhaps the politest man in the history of mankind. I'd booked this place mainly because of websites such as Trip Advisor, which unanimously ranked it the best hotel in Thamel, Kathmandu's lively tourist district.

'I will carry your bag upstairs, sir,' he told me after all the formalities were out of the way.

'That's ok, mate,' I answered him. 'I need the exercise, I'll carry it.'

He gave me a look that cried sorrowfulness, picked my bag up and looked at me with puppy-dog eyes, as if asking permission to take it, just as the photographer at the airport had done with his bribe not more than two hours before. I smiled and gave him the smallest of nods. He returned my smile three-fold, and within two seconds he was up the stairs and out of sight, while I tried my hardest not to be out of breath at this most mediocre of tasks.

I like tipping people in the poor places of the world that I visit. The gratefulness and smiles that I receive make it all worthwhile. I knew I didn't have any Nepali currency and that the smallest note I had to give this man was $5 US for carrying my bag upstairs; so once he had shown me the room, which was immaculate, comfortable, and exactly like the pictures on the internet, I held out the note for him. He bowed his head and thanked me, but left without taking the money. I don't know why. Perhaps he was embarrassed to take so much money for such a simple task. Perhaps he carried the bag out of the kindness of his own heart, and it wasn't in fact in his job description. I stared at the back of the door in amazement. I turned and did a bad impression of the Fosbury Flop right onto the bed, which was so hard that it seemed as though the designers had taken their inspiration from a slab of cement. It literally knocked the wind out of me and I felt like I'd been hit by a falling tree.

'What the f...' I began to say, but never got to finish the sentence as I was already fast asleep.

Chapter Two

HAVING A WANDER

I awoke with golden sunshine streaming in through an unclosed slit in the curtains. I had a blanket over me, but was horrified to find that I was soaking wet (It was sweat. I know, you thought I'd pissed myself!). I had set the air conditioner on the coldest setting when I'd gone to sleep, but now an eerie silence filled the room. I fumbled around for the remote control, found it, then pressed the on/off button repeatedly but the damn thing was dead.

I went to switch on my lamp. It was dead. TV – dead. I had no power in my room. I was as groggy as could be and in no mood to move, so I went and opened my window and collapsed back onto my bed. I drifted in and out of consciousness for a while, before being brought back to reality by two short, sharp beeps, announcing the air conditioner coming back on and the end to my first Kathmandu power cut.

*

I had come to Nepal to trek the Himalayas, but more specifically to undertake the challenging 'Three Passes Trek', as it has become known. I had a whole month, so I wanted to 'walk' into the mountains through the foothills of the Himalaya, starting at a small town called Jiri, a day's bus ride from Kathmandu. Many trekkers now fly directly into the mountains to a place called Lukla at an altitude of 2860m (9380ft), landing on a short, steep runway carved into the face of a mountain. Having done a bit of research into acute mountain sickness (AMS) and the type of fitness these three passes would require of me, I decided that walking in from Jiri was the best idea. The seven-day trek to Lukla would take me *up and down*, *up and down*, all day, every day. Climbing up ridges before dropping down into the next valley, and then repeating.

It didn't sound like the most fun in the world, but it was necessary. In the course of seven days, I would ascend to a maximum altitude of 3530m (11581ft) over the Lamjura Pass (a good 1300m higher than Australia's highest mountain, Mount Kosciuszko), which would get the altitude acclimatisation ball rolling. It was still some way short of my highest intended point of the trek, the Kongma La Pass at 5535m (18160ft). But anyway, I'm jumping the gun. First I had to find some poor soul to guide me there, and have someone agree to carry my bag for me.

I'd decided to wing it, so I'd organised absolutely nothing before leaving Australia with the exception of the room in Kathmandu for two nights; my rationale being that a huge part of this poor country's economy was based on tourism, so there would be plenty of people willing to take me. I was getting a little excited lying in bed and thinking about what the new day might hold, so I leapt up, showered, dressed and left my room. I bounded down the stairs with the enthusiasm of a man on a mission.

The same man was at reception and he greeted me with an even bigger smile than the night before.

'Good morning, sir!' he said with the utmost sincerity in his voice.

'Good morning! Don't you sleep or what?' I asked him. He checked me in a little after midnight and it was fast approaching 10am.

'No, sir! I mean yes, sir, but not much of the sleeps. You will be having the breakfast?'

'Absolutely!' I replied a little eagerly. 'I love breakfast.'

The man laughed as though I was Billy Connolly and he was being treated to a private show. It was contagious, so I joined in.

After a good few minutes he regained his composure and said, 'This way please, sir.'

He directed me about four metres away to the entrance of the restaurant. It was small and homely and was joined onto the lobby. In charge was a very small man with a lovely smile and limited English speaking capabilities; but a genuine smile transcends the boundaries of language, and I knew this man was a good, kind human being.

'Eggs, sir?' He asked me.

'Yes please.'

'Toast, sir?

'I'd love some,' I answered him, but a confused look clouded his face. 'Yes please,' I added quickly and he gave me a look of recognition that was enveloped by a massive smile.

'Tea, sir?'

'Yes, please. White.'

'Yes, sir. Thank you, sir. Please, this is buffet,' he added while pointing to five or so silver thingies that cover hot food at buffets. Alas, I know not the name of them. My little friend wandered off to the adjoining kitchen segregated from the dining room by a large, glass window, and called the order in to the chef. I love a large, glass window so that you can see the chef not spitting in your eggs.

There were some interesting things under those silver thingies. Potatoes, capsicum, plain noodles, but one of them had some kind of a fish pakora underneath it. I wasn't quite sure how I felt about that at any time of the day, let alone for breakfast. But nonetheless I carefully rounded up two pieces with a dessert spoon and put them next to my plate of steaming potatoes and green capsicum.

Of the eight tables, only two were being occupied. Seated at one was a lone male traveller of Scandinavian descent, while at the other sat two middle-aged German women. I walked to the back of the room and took a seat facing back into the dining room, and then just kind of sat there and eye-balled the fish. It stared back at me, and seemed to say, 'Go on, I dare ya!'

Did I dare?

As I sat in silent contemplation, a 20-something-year-old red-haired girl with a slightly green face walked into the dining room and announced herself as an Aussie with a thickly accented greeting to the little man.

'Good morning madam,' he said. 'Eggs, madam?'

'Oh God no!' she replied. 'I'm sick, food poisoning,' she added while rubbing her stomach.

'Toast?'

'Yes, ok.'

I stared at my plate with renewed suspicion. Was it the fish that made the girl sick? I wanted to ask her, but she sat and put her head straight down onto the table. She stayed there long enough to get a whiff of egg, before bolting back from whence she had come.

Kathmandu has been food poisoning people for years, so did I dare eat a fish in a land-locked country with appalling hygiene standards? Where did that fish come from?

I moved my fork towards it, but at the last possible second I wimped out and took a detour for a piece of potato and capsicum. I ate that, and then was about to try again when I noticed my little mate bringing my cup of tea; so I put my cutlery down and watched him arrive, thanked him, and returned my death-stare to the poor little bit of fish.

Next to me the Scandinavian dude had wolfed down his plate and before you could cast a lure he was up and heading back to the buffet table. I watched with interest to see what he was going for, but was shocked when he only opened the silver thingy with the fish pakora under it. He piled his plate high with fish. He loved it.

Just do it you pansy... a voice inside my head mocked me, so I just did it. Well, it was probably the most delicious fish I had ever eaten. The pakora batter was perfectly crunchy, and once I got into the fish, it wasn't really the *fishy* fish that I had feared, but a lovely *meaty* fish, like a Spanish Mackerel or a Barramundi. Encased in that little parcel of crunchy batter were delicious flavours of lemon, coriander and other subcontinental spices of the most wonderful complexity. I smiled as widely as my little mate had done minutes before and then went and loaded my plate up with the last of the fish pakoras. When I was back at my seat I noticed the man lift the lids of the silver thingies, systematically checking them, and he almost fell over when he saw there was nothing in the fish bowl. I can't imagine what was going through his head, but I think, 'You greedy bastards!' would have been about right.

I ate about five fishes, forgetting that I had toast and eggs on the way; and with wasting food in Nepal about as well received as a fart in an elevator, I had to finish it all. Good thing I love breakfast.

*

I took to the streets of Thamel, firstly to get a feel for the place, and secondly to find a guide and porter. I was meant to be leaving for my trek the following day. I exited the narrow lane and joined the circus that is Kathmandu. Motorbikes hooned around, beeping their horns furiously at pedestrians forced to share the road due to a lack of footpaths. Dust was thrown into the air from every single moving atom. Thick, unprotected and dangerously tangled power lines drooped to almost-touching height. Prayer flags suspended across the streets from building to building flapped rhythmically in the breeze, while matching colourful signs

20

overhanging the roads announced an abundance of trekking gear shops and trekking agencies. Music shops played the same song, over and over again. It was Buddhist chanting music, with a choir of monks singing the mantra 'Om Mani Pädme Hum' in angelic voices. I felt very privileged to be walking around this ancient city, and this music certainly gave me a very spiritual sensation that I find hard to describe.

Everything was named after the great Himalayan Mountains. I snapped a photo of a particularly chaotic street, and examining it later that evening I counted the name 'Everest' on 14 different signs, from banks to restaurants to trekking agencies. Poor Sir George Everest would be turning in his grave. He objected to the mountain being named after him, and was actually quite embarrassed by the association, but the Royal Geographical Society went ahead with it anyway. Mount Everest to us, *Sagarmatha* or 'forehead in the sky' to the Nepalese, and *Chomolungma* or 'mother of mountains' in Tibet (although I have also heard it translated as 'goddess mother of the world', which I secretly prefer). And a little fun fact for you: We're all mispronouncing Everest. George's last name was pronounced Eve-rest, as in the girl's name. So imagine the sentence,

'Eve had a rest.' Now read only the first and last word of the previous sentence. I like to imagine old George would be quite happy about that.

I walked around for hours, trying not to get lost in the maze of streets that followed absolutely no recognisable pattern. In my part of the world we are very boring, building everything in the grid system, where streets either run parallel or at a 90-degree angle to each other. Boring, but very hard to get lost. Here there was no system and everything looked the same and was called the same thing. I found myself lost and thinking, *Now this looks familiar, there is the New Himalayan Lodge! Oh no wait, it was the Old Himalayan Lodge I saw before. Ah wait, there's the Everest Tibetan Guesthouse from earlier... or was it the Everest Buddhist Guesthouse I'm thinking of?*

I was approached by a young fellow claiming to be a student of English looking to have a friendly chat with me.

'Ah no worries mate,' I'd answered him. 'What university do you study at?'

Well he couldn't even come up with a single one. If he'd said the Everest Himalayan University I may just have believed him.

'What are you selling?' I asked him now, all the friendliness having evaporated from my voice.

'Nothing, my friend, I am just a students.'

'You are a student that doesn't know the name of your school? Not too clever, ay?'

'Where are you from, man?' He tried to change the subject.

'I'm from Australia where we don't like bull-shitters.'

'Ah Australia, mate!' He tried to cheer me up.

He followed and tried to chat to me for a good few miles. He was a persistent little bugger, despite me having sussed him out in about three seconds.

After perhaps 15 minutes (and still dumber than dog shit), he said, 'So my friend, because I am the poor students, maybe I be your guide in the Kathmandu for one day, and maybe you could be paying me $25. This is a win–win no?'

'No.'

'Yes, my friend, is a wins.'

'No mate, I'm not your friend,' I said, which is something only an Aussie could say and get away with. 'You are lying to me, I don't trust you and I hate you, now piss off.'

You may think I was perhaps a touch rude, but he had hassled me for 15 minutes. I know blokes that would have just belted him.

I'd gone into a couple of agencies to enquire about guides and porters, but honestly I picked up a bad vibe from all of them. They were salesmen, whereas I needed someone personable. They were the kind of people that followed you down the road even after you said you weren't interested and that you were going to find someone else. I hate that. Forgive the cliché, but this was the trip of a lifetime for me and I needed a good, English speaking guide and a reliable porter. I remembered something the taxi driver had mentioned the night before, that the hotel I was staying at could arrange a trek for me.

I was developing a pretty severe headache, an unusual phenomenon for me, so I knew I'd been out and about for too long. The dust I'd been swallowing and inhaling all day, combined with perhaps a bit of jet-lag was beginning to take its toll. I headed back to the hotel, slightly dejected that I'd not arranged a single thing.

*

As I approached the hotel, the darkly tinted doors, impenetrable to the human gaze, mysteriously opened and I was greeted by my two friends, the restaurant man and the reception man. I feel slightly aggrieved to not mention their names, but if truth be told, I am so terrible with names that I have absolutely no idea what they are. I once had a man work under me for two weeks before I was confident enough to call him anything else other than 'mate'!

Their collective smiles told me I was home. Hotel Friend's Home. Their motto is, 'Come as a guest and leave as a friend.' Isn't that sweet? It is quite a hard mantra to live up to, but those guys do it naturally, with ease.

'How was your walking, sir?' enquired the receptionist.

'It was fantastic!' I told him truthfully. 'But you have too many English students. Maybe 20 people tell me they are students!'

'Ah yes, sir. They is not really the students.'

'Yeah I know. What are you doing anyway? Pulling a 15-hour shift? Don't you sleep?

He laughed uncontrollably.

'Yes sir,' he finally answered. 'I am working a long day, but then I get the long time to not be working.'

'Ok mate, I'm just worried about you.'

'No need to worry, sir. You want a cup of tea?'

'I would love one. And also I have a couple of questions about trekking for you if that's ok?'

He clapped his hands together once and muttered something very quickly to the restaurant boss, who scurried off as quick as a flash.

'Please, have a seat, sir,' he said, offering an open hand towards the small leather lounge suite located just inside the main door. My cup of tea arrived just as my bum was hitting the seat and I sipped at it furiously, destroying it in seconds. My receptionist mate had gone off to grab the manager, who came out just as I was taking my last sip.

'Good afternoon, sir!' He said in flawless English, introducing himself in the process; but alas, I'm hopeless. God knows why, but whenever someone says their name, a brass band begins playing in my head for exactly the amount of time it takes to say their name. 'My name is (cue brass band!) and I am the manager here. How may I assist you?'

'Actually I am looking to go on a trek and I heard you can help me. I was looking to go tomorrow, but I understand that it is now very short notice, so the next day is no problem.'

'My friend, if you want to go this very second, it would not be a problem.'

'I'm a bit tired mate, but tomorrow would be awesome.'

'Ok, please you are tired. Go to your room now and rest. I will get my tourism manager on the phone and tell him to come and meet you here, and I will have my receptionist phone for you once he is here. Is that ok for you?'

I was as happy as a pig in shit.

'That would be fine,' I answered, thinking I'd somehow been transported to The Waldorf Astoria.

'Is there anything else I can do for you, sir?' he asked.

'There is just one more thing,' I answered him, with what I'm sure was a glimmer in my eye. 'Could I have an Everest Beer to take up to my room please?'

As his receptionist had done earlier, he barked a few quick words to the restaurant guy, and within seconds I had a cold Everest Beer in my grasp and was making my way back to the comfort of my room.

It was surprisingly tasty, the Everest Beer. I didn't have my expectations too high, which probably worked in my favour. It was beer, it was wet and I was parched! I finished it, taking a couple of selfies in the process, before remembering I had my duty-free rum sitting innocently in a plastic bag by my suitcase. It was a bottle of Bacardi 8, aged 8 years. This is quite a nice sipping rum, so I poured a little into a glass and began sipping. I was about to embark on an arduous journey (just how arduous, I didn't know) so these comforts were absolutely necessary.

I'd been upstairs for perhaps only 20 minutes when the phone rang, announcing the arrival of the Tourism Manager.

Chapter Three

HIRING A GUIDE

Rammani Rijial, the manager of Outdoor Himalayan Treks, was sitting behind the small desk that sat in the small lobby. He looked to be somewhere between his late twenties and early thirties, was of medium build and had a slightly chubby face which lent him a friendly, charismatic kind of appearance. The kind of face a caricature artist would have a lot of fun drawing. He wore a suit and was very presentable. I liked him before I knew him.

'Mr. Alexander, it is a pleasure to meet you,' he said with sincerity. 'My colleagues here tell me you are interested in some trekking in our beautiful Nepal.'

'I sure am. I'd like to do the Three Passes Trek, but starting from Jiri.'

We sat down and flogged out the details - how long it would take, the altitude acclimatisation days I would need, the costs of the guide and porter per day, what was included in the final price and what wasn't. It was all very clear and professional, with no hidden charges. I liked that.

'Have you any questions for me?' he enquired after finishing his speech.

'Yes I do. I need assurances that the guide is a young man that speaks very good English.'

'You will have the guide Subash (pronounced Su-bass), he is 24 and has the very good English.'

'He has done the Three Passes before?'

'Many, many times.'

'When would we leave?'

'You would leave tomorrow morning from this hotel at 5.30am, with the bus leaving for Jiri from Ratna Park Bus Station at 7am.'

'Ok. I heard that some of the passes were closed because of snow.'

'Yes this is true, but it will be two weeks from now when you come to the first pass. Should be no problem.'

'Ok. So do I have to do anything this afternoon?'

'Mr Alex, we will buy your bus ticket from the money you pay us, we will sort out all your permits; we will do everything. I will come back here this evening to introduce you to your guide. Now do you have good boots? Do you need anything?'

'I just need a good sleeping bag.'

'Ok we can hire you one for five dollars per day.'

'Ok, done. I'm happy, where do I sign?'

Rammani clapped his hands together once and uttered a quick word to his assistant who quickly brought over the credit card machine.

'I will call to you in a couple of hours when everything is booked and I will bring you the guide.'

The day was getting old, and I was fast becoming exhausted. I had completed every single task I had set for myself. So I retired to my room once more for a couple more rums.

Realising I was in yet another blackout session, I opened my window to Kathmandu. Directly below me was a construction site that seemed to be some kind of barracks for dozens of armed soldiers, with assault rifles and bullet proof vests which read the letters 'A.P.F.'. Thousands of crows – or maybe they were ravens – had taken to the darkening evening sky, as though they were bats. Looking further still I saw a rectangular park with green grass that could quite reasonably have been a rugby or a soccer pitch, but instead it was being used as a car park. Kathmandu is just too crowded.

On the other side of the park a main road hummed with vehicles of all shapes and sizes, beeping their horns relentlessly as a warning to pedestrians that shared the roads. A large, ancient, Tibetan-style building a few miles away reflected the final ray of sunshine that this day was ever going to give. Further still, the beginning of the mighty Langtang mountain ranges, with its peaks standing tall like sentries, the guardians of the Kathmandu Valley.

The ring of the phone snapped me from my rum-induced day dream, with the man on the other end telling me that Mr Rammani and Mr Subash were here to see me. I bounded down the stairs once more and saw Subash Gurung for the first time; a handsome-looking man, very slight in stature and probably only 5 foot 5 inches in height, with a big head of hair and with some definite Mongolian heritage. These features prompted a pair of Aussie travellers I would meet later on to nickname him 'Bollywood'.

'And here is a gift for you,' Rammani said, throwing me a sleeping bag.

'Ah thanks,' I replied, genuinely warmed by his smile.

'A gift you must give back,' he said a little more seriously. 'On the 26th of March,' a little more seriously still.

'Yep, that's what renting is,' I laughed before the situation became awkward.

I shook hands with Subash and exchanged a few words, but Rammani was understandably keen to get going, so we said good night and called it a day. I cautiously climbed onto the slab, and was asleep within seconds.

*

The following morning found me sitting in the lobby nice and early next to a Sherpa man, drinking a cup of tea. He kept looking at me, that Sherpa man, so eventually I turned to him to wish him 'good morning'. It must have been early, because I didn't put two and two together.

'Hello, good morning,' I greeted the man.

'Ah, the good morning, sir!' he responded quickly in broken English, and he began to get very excited. 'I am the Nima, sir! From bang ti gangly wang Makalu region, sir!'

'Ah, very good,' I replied, as I'm sure a look of recognition began to take hold of my face. 'Oh my God, you're my porter aren't you?'

'Yes is porter, sir!'

'I am Gordon. Good to meet you,' I told him while standing up to shake his hand. He took my hand with his, and then enclosed it completely with his other hand and begun shaking it furiously, while an ear-to-ear smile caused many wrinkles to form on his neck, cheeks and brow. Nima was a proud Sherpa porter from the Makalu region of Nepal. He stretched barely five feet off the ground, had short black hair and tremendously big ears; but he had a smile that would have made a dictator want to play with a puppy.

I'd read too much about Sherpa people to doubt this man would have any problem carrying my bag.

Subash came bundling through the door, crying, 'Oh Mr Alex! A good morning to you. I see you have met the Nima.'

'Yes I met the Nima,' I laughed, in spite of myself.

Subash barked a command to Nima, who jumped up, poor thing, without finishing his cup of tea and ran over and picked up my backpack.

'It's not too heavy for him?' I asked Subash.

'For the Nima? No ways man! He is strong Sherpa from Makalu region. Nothing is a too heavy for the Nima.'

We piled into the tiny taxi that Subash had arrived in, but I was rather taken aback, to say the least, when he jumped into the front seat. I was a great deal taller than Subash – I'm 6 foot 3 and rather chunky – and I presumed that as his employer he'd let me have the leg room, but instead I found myself in the back with squashed nads and my ankles around my ears.

Wouldn't be a good start to upset him in the first minute, I thought, so I bit my tongue and watched Kathmandu greet the new morning.

After a while we pulled up at a wide open area, jam-packed with buses of all shapes, sizes and colours. Nima grabbed my pack and mounted it onto his back with ease, while Subash took off for a distant corner of the station. It is a very strange sensation, at first, to have someone carry all your stuff for you. I am a big, strong man that has worked in manual labour intensive jobs, so I wasn't used to having someone help me out to such an extent, and certainly not a man almost twice my age and half my size! However, I was giving a poor man a job and it did feel good.

I immediately needed the toilet (you can't take me anywhere) which I relayed to Subash.

'You is needing the pee pee or the poo poo?' he asked, deadly serious.

'The pee pee,' I said, while having to use every ounce of my strength to prevent the corners of my lips from raising into a smile, which I was certain would lead to uncontrollable laughter. I had to nip it in the bud. He peeled off a few rupee notes and handed them to me.

'Is a different price for the pee pee and the poo poos.'

I made a snorting noise from my nose, but this time it was too much and I broke into laughter.

'What is funny?' He asked, genuinely bemused by me finding that so funny.

'Nothing, nothing,' I finally managed to say. 'In Australia we say 'piss' and 'shit', but what you said makes sense.'

'Ah, piss and shit?'

'Yeah, piss and shit.'

'Ok, toilet over there, the Nima will show you.'

The toilet was revolting, and I've seen some pretty bad toilets in my time; at service stations in Jordan, in some remote areas of Saudi Arabia, and just most toilets in Egypt. This one was definitely in the ball park. *I couldn't do a poo poo in here, even if I wanted to,* I pondered to myself while holding my breath.

'We are thirty minutes too much early,' Subash told me as I re-joined him. 'Tea?'

We entered a dirty little café where only the locals went. A small boy no more than 7 or 8 years old with grubby hands brought us three glasses of steamy, milky tea. The smell that came off that tea resembled, I imagine, a spice market in an Indian city. It smelt glorious. I sipped eagerly and was slapped in the face by cardamom, cinnamon and cloves, then by nutmeg and rich brown sugar. My eyes widened, as if I'd solved the deepest mysteries of the universe. This was the single nicest cup of tea I had ever had. Without doubt and without peer. At a grubby little café in Ratna Park Bus Station in Kathmandu. If you want to look for it, it is the one closest to the toilets!

*

'This is our buses,' Subash told me while pointing to a modern, white mini-van that was pulling into the station. 'Come.'

'How do you know?' I asked him, genuinely interested, as there was absolutely nothing to discern this bus from the 274 other identical buses sprawled around the place.

'Because I am the very good Nepali trekking guide!' he scolded me, a little offended.

I had much to learn.

Nima threw my backpack up to a boy of probably only 10 years, who caught it without straining and tied everything down with a rope. I kept my day pack with my camera and Snickers bars with me. We scrambled to the back row and Subash ushered me to the window seat. Excellent for seeing things, atrocious for leg room. I was squashed and uncomfortable and we hadn't even pulled out of the station yet.

'How long is this bus journey?' I enquired politely of my guide.

'It is very much depending on the road's conditions,' he replied. 'Could be the six hours, maybe is the 13 hours. Sometimes there is the mud slides on the roads and so maybe it be two days.'

Should have flown into Lukla, I thought, before snapping myself out of it.

We began to roll, then the boy slammed a cassette into the tape player, blaring out hideous Nepali music so loud that the speakers began to crackle under the strain.

'Oh my dear, sweet Jesus,' I said out loud, but they were words no one was ever to hear. Instead a bus full of Nepali people, including my guide and porter, had broken into chorus, all of them singing the same, atrocious, whiney song. I smiled and tried to join in. This would never happen back home, after all.

We made our way slowly out of a gridlocked Kathmandu, never hitting more than 40km/h. In fact travelling at 40km/h felt exhilaratingly quick. Everywhere people just kind of stood around the streets, talking to each other. Hundreds and hundreds of people.

'Why are there so many people, just *doing nothing*?' I shouted my question to Subash.

'They is not having the jobs. They is having nowhere to go in the day.'

Almost half of Nepal's labour-force is without jobs. The number is about 46% (according to Wikipedia's 'List of countries by unemployment rate'), ranking it the ninth highest in the world; a little better than Senegal, but not as good as Kosovo. No wonder so many people had nothing to do. No wonder the streets were always crowded with people just standing around. It was terribly sad to see, even if the people did not seem particularly unhappy. Their existence was nothing new to them, as it was to me.

The man sitting in front of me cracked his window open, initially to my delight, but unfortunately he was letting a great deal of dust into the bus. We slammed down narrow streets, jumped over pot-holes, narrowly avoided cows, men, women and children, dodged piles of rubble inexplicably blocking sections of road, and came across policemen pretending to be traffic lights, all the while inhaling dangerous volumes of dust.

Before long we began to rise out of the valley and I caught a glimpse of something huge. It was a statue, high up on the hills. Catching my expression, Subash informed me that it was in fact a statue of Lord Shiva, a deity in the Hindu religion. It was called the Kailashnath Mahadev Statue and was, in fact, the single tallest statue of Lord Shiva in the world. It stands at 44m (143ft) from the ground and is the world's 40th largest statue. To put it into perspective, the Statue of Liberty is the world's 36th tallest statue, and it is only 2 metres taller than this statue of Lord Shiva (Thanks Wikipedia, you bloody ripper!). Copper in colour, the god stood proudly with a trident in the left hand, the other hand held up vertically with the palm facing outwards in a sign of peace. Coiled around the neck was a cobra, which rose to a striking stance on the right shoulder so that both Shiva's and the snake's eyes were at the same height. I was taken aback by this unexpected monolith, and I turned my head slowly around to keep the god in my gaze until eventually an inevitably it disappeared from view.

'Wow,' I said to myself as we began to wind our way up the side of a large hill. We went through a small town where children played badminton on the side of the road, old men tested each other's skills in a board game I had never seen before, puppies played and young boys tried to stop the bus to sell the white man a bottle of water, or some strange looking sweets that I had never seen before. The scenery was immensely beautiful. Rolling green hills gave way to sharper inclines and jagged ridge tops, which then returned again to rolling hills. All of which we had to negotiate in a little bus on a single lane road while dodging everything from motorbikes to trucks firing at us from the opposite direction. Often the edge of the road marked the beginning of the cliff with a vertical drop for hundreds, if not thousands of feet to the bottom of the valley. Unnerving? Nay, it was petrifying!

Our driver had obviously driven this road a million times, yet over-confidence often is the cause of accidents and we came millimetres from hitting cows, people and oncoming traffic on numerous occasions. He would attempt to overtake trucks on the steepest inclines on the blindest of corners, and his sole safety net was to beep his horn continuously, as if to say, 'Slow down! Can't you see I'm overtaking you on a blind corner and we could be seconds away from death if you don't let me go around you?' Man it was scary. It took a great and unnatural willpower to tear my gaze off of the road and back onto the breathtaking scenery.

At about 10am the bus suddenly pulled over on the side of the road at a rare area of even ground.

'It is time to make the pee pee, Mr Alex.'

I started to make a snorting noise again. I know, I'm immature, but I can't help it. All the men in the bus filed out and to my complete interest, they all formed a line, shoulder to shoulder, and began to urinate in the same spot on the ground. I shrugged my shoulders and joined in. When in Nepal...

*

As the ride commenced we passed numerous police check points where everything from my passport to my TIMS (Trekker's Information Management System – something a trekker needs to enter protected areas in Nepal, arranged by the trekking agency before we left) card was checked.

'What's with all the police check-points?' I asked Subash when we were on our way again for about the fifth time.

'This is the road to China, so many checks. Maybe there is being some illegal peoples.'

Eventually we came grinding to a halt once more, but this time everyone got out of the bus. Subash announced it to be lunchtime by putting all his fingers together and raising them to his mouth.

The restaurant had open walls and was called something like The Himalayan View Restaurant, which wouldn't have been far wrong. We were suspended high up on the side of a mountain and the restaurant afforded glorious views into the valley below. I was excited. I was about to get my first hit of Dal Bhat, the national dish of Nepal. Simply translated as 'rice and lentils', it is a very cheap and nutritious meal for the poor people of Nepal.

We sat down on long, lineal, wooden benches and waited for the food to arrive. We didn't have to wait long. An empty plate was placed in front of me, which an elderly lady loaded up with steaming white rice from a communal pot. First me, then Subash, then Nima. She brought out a bowl of lentil soup, a different bowl of turmeric-coloured curried potatoes, some green beans and some pickle thing that was so hot it numbed my tongue and turned my nose into a waterfall. I watched the locals to see how it was done before having a go myself. Subash poured the soup over the rice – not all of it you see, but just the perfect amount to give the rice the perfect consistency to eat it with your hands – then loaded the plate with the curried potatoes and a little bit of the pickled chillies.

The cutest little four-year-old waiter brought out a spoon for me and held it up while hiding his face out of shyness. I caught his attention, gave him a little bow to say thank you, then gave him the same gesture that Subash had done to me nearly 10 minutes before, telling him I would be eating with my hands today. He smiled and ran off to the kitchen to return the spoon. I noticed that everyone else at the table was smiling as well, giving me the impression that most foreigners would have taken the spoon. I am pretty good at eating with my hands, having lived in Jordan for six months; but I poured way too much soup on the rice and it became a sloppy mess. But it was absolutely delicious, despite my rookie mistake.

The old lady brought out seconds for everyone, which everyone partook in. When she came around a third time I became a little anxious because I was entirely stuffed. She went to put more rice on Subash's plate, but I noticed him put his hand over his plate and shook it slightly, preventing the lady from filling

45

him up. I quickly duplicated his action as the lady attempted to fatten me up some more. Nima had thirds. God knows where he put it all. It cost me 110 Nepalese rupees ($1.10 US).

The restaurant had two outdoor sinks that we lined up to wash our hands at, and the pressure of the water took me by surprise. It bounced off the bottom of the sink and straight onto my crotch, then unfortunately for me I went to the toilet. While I was in there another bus had pulled up and out jumped six European girls and a couple of guys.

Then I came out of the toilet.

'Ah Alex man!' Exclaimed Subash, so loud that everyone within a one-mile radius could hear. 'You pissed on your pants!'

I looked down, mortified, then defended myself, 'No, that's from the sink!'

'It is looking like the piss, man.'

'How can you tell the difference?'

He looked at me for a little while, then muttered, 'Mmmm ok,' but I could tell he didn't believe me.

*

The further we distanced ourselves from Kathmandu the more the roads disintegrated.

By the time we were descending the valley into Jiri, we were bouncing up and down and banging our heads on the roof. Such was the state of the road that we had slowed to a crawl. I looked across and was dumbfounded to find that Nima was fast asleep and his little body was getting thrown around. Then I looked at the man sitting next to him, who was far from happy. Nima had slipped right over and was now fast asleep on the poor guy's shoulder, but he was too polite to do anything about it.

I made eye contact with him and made a motion as if to say, 'Bash him with your elbow and he'll move'. The man's face burst into a grin and to my amusement he jammed his elbow in Nima's ribs, as if getting permission from Nima's employer was all he needed to go for it. The Nima woke up briefly and opened and closed his mouth a couple of times before his head lolled back to sleep up against the head rest. I exchanged a brief 'thumbs up' and a smile with the man before returning my view to life in the hills.

On the side of the road, men and women were busy clearing drains by sweeping leaves into a pile and then setting them on fire, therefore filling the hills with light-blue smoke. As we groaned our way over the final ridge it began to hail, the noise of which on the tin roof was almost deafening.

I felt a tap on my shoulder, followed by a finger pointing to somewhere distant, where I could make out a series of buildings with sky-blue rooves and other houses built on terraces carved into the hills.

'Jiri,' was all Subash said.

Nine hours after setting off we pulled into Jiri, a town that I had been reading about for a decade and the original starting point for many of the great mountaineering expeditions attempting to conquer Everest for the first time.

Chapter Four

LET THE TREK BEGIN

We trundled across the road and announced our arrival at the Sherpa Guest House Restaurant and Lodge. The lady in charge was in her mid-thirties, was a Sherpa and was fairly over-weight, but just loved having us stay for the company and gossip. She took us up some steep, creaky old stairs and showed me where I was to spend the night. Two small single beds lined the walls of a fairly spacious room. I walked over to one of the beds and sat down. I thought perhaps the mattress was made from granite rock, but I'd already spent two nights on a slab of cement, so granite wasn't going to faze me too much.

I looked at Subash, who had a worried look on his face.

'What's wrong mate?' I asked him.

'Is the room fine for you Alex? If not we could be going somewhere else.'

'The room is perfect mate. No problems. All good.'

'You are sure?'

'Yes I'm sure! Stop asking me. Everything is good.'

'OK,' he answered slowly and a little uneasily. I didn't know it at the time, because I'd only really known Subash for 10 hours, but it was a sign of his professionalism as a guide that he wanted to make sure I was perfectly happy with his service right from the beginning. He could have taken me to any number of lodges scattered throughout Jiri, but they would have all been similar. The room was as basic as could be, but it was also perfectly adequate - and clean. What more could you ask for in the middle of nowhere?

We went up another flight of creaky stairs into the dining room, which had maps and mountaineering memorabilia plastered all over the walls.

'You want to go for the walks?' Subash asked me.

'Yeah ok, I need some exercise.'

We made our way back down the stairs and out onto the street. Jiri had many trekking shops, but I didn't see a single tourist in Jiri other than myself. In its heyday, Jiri was a bustling epicentre for all things trekking, but it has been in a steady decline ever since the opening of the airport in Lukla. Even the road doesn't conclude at Jiri anymore, but carries on to the next town of Shivalaya (where we were hiking to the following day); and it is even possible to catch a lift along a muddy goat-track to the next town of Bhandar if you so choose to, but what would be the point in that?

We made our way down the cobbled street and veered off onto a muddy track, coming across a gang of six men working with the most primitive of tools on some drainage system across the path. As we got to within 150 metres of them, they all stopped work, put down their tools and stared at me with expressionless faces. I felt a little uneasy, to be honest. I smiled and said 'hello' as I passed, but their expressions remained unchanged. *I could probably take five of them,* I joked to myself. *But six, that's tough!* I watch a lot of Kung Fu.

We did a little loop and then began to climb for the very first time up the side of a hill towards a Buddhist shrine, perhaps only 40 vertical metres above the town.

Well I was hopelessly out of shape. Jiri was only 2100m (6890 ft) above sea level and the oxygen was plentiful, but within a few seconds I was breathing deeply and my heart was racing. I was trying very hard to breathe as silently as possible so as not to alert Subash of my conditioning. I was only half way up and needed a rest, but I wasn't going to let on. I stopped, took out my camera and began taking some photos of nothing in particular.

At the top sat a golden Buddha and I was intrigued to note that in his left hand was the same three-pronged trident that Lord Shiva was holding. Subash's religious knowledge wasn't his strongest asset, so I vowed to do some research into the matter when I returned to civilisation.

We made our way back to the lodge and sat upstairs in the communal dining room.

'Right, who wants a beer?' I asked the boys, but they stared sheepishly at the floor. 'Come on, it's ok, first day of the trek so I am buying the beers.' They smiled and accepted my offer so we ordered three Everest Beers. To my horror the lady went to the cupboard to get them, not a fridge as I had imagined.

'Subash, ask her if she has any cold beers mate.'

'Yes is having. Why you want the cold beer?'

'All beer should be cold. Ice cold,' I answered him, not able to believe I was having this conversation.

'No ways man. Nepal is a cold country so we like the warm beer.'

I shook my head in disgust. I wanted to put my fingers in my ears and say 'la la la la la' over and over again to drown out the noise. Where I'm from, serving someone a warm beer is punishable by death.

My beer arrived and it was just cold enough to drink. We had several of them, and I even tried a Nepali bitter called Gurkha, but it was putrid and one sip was all I needed. So I jumped back on the Everest Beer and we drank until we were merry.

'Yo Alex man are you bored?' Subash asked me after a moment of silence.

'No mate I'm not bored.'

'No man, not bored – bald?'

'That's a strange question, but yeah, slowly,' I said while pointing to the top of my head.

He burst out laughing, then said, a little exasperated, 'No man! Cored!'

'Am I cored? What does that mean?' It was my turn to get a little exasperated. Subash's English had gone to shit after a couple of beverages. 'Ah you mean cold?'

'Yes!'

'No I'm not cold.'

And we went into a fit of laughter. I think it was the Everest beer talking.

*

I was having quite a pleasant sleep until about 1am. I was awoken by someone booting me in the guts. I quickly realised that it had been a dream, but the pain had not gone away. I needed the dunny, big style. Now, let me point out that, including the family that ran the lodge, there were only seven of us staying under that roof.

I saw out the gripe, and waited, hoping in vain that it was a one-off. They never are. I

54

heard footsteps stir in the room above me. They headed for the stairs and then, with a sense of dread, I realised that they were going to use the only toilet. Something from deep down inside me gurgled. And then the second wave hit me with exponential force. *Why didn't you go the first time you fool!*

I had a stressful eight minutes forty-two seconds there, but I managed to hold on. Before I'd even finished my business, I heard the steps again and the latch to the toilet started to rattle. The person on the other side of the door was probably thinking – *What a coincidence, fancy the toilet being busy at this time of night!*

As it turned out it was Nima. Both times.

'Good morning, Nima,' I greeted him, back in the dining area the next morning.

'Ah morning sir,' he said.

'You sleep well?' I asked.

'Ah yes sir, but then no sir. I awaken up a maybe one morning time with direa'. Waking up a many times sir. Been high altitude working and then back Kathmandu. Drank a chang pin dup gul traga then last night more beer. All mix in stom and no good sir.'

'Ah no good,' I said, not really knowing what to say, but he seemed pleased with my response. This was one of the times I actually knew what he was talking about, and I'm sure he sensed this. I certainly think that sometimes he looks at me during his speeches and thinks: *This guy has no idea what I'm talking about.*

Subash joined us and we ordered breakfast. I ordered what was known as the 'Set Breakfast', which was about six times more expensive than any other option. *This must be huge,* I reasoned. Well the set breakfast is scrambled eggs, fried potato and four pieces of crummy toast. I could have made the same thing from the menu for at least half the price. Then I did a quick conversion into Australian dollars, and told myself to stop whinging. It was about three bucks.

'Thank you – *darnaybaad,*' I said to my hosts.

'You're welcome, enjoy your trekking,' they said.

Then we were off.

I strapped on my boots for the first time in Nepal, before hitting the literal road to Shivalaya, following it out of town for perhaps a kilometre, before veering off onto a well-trodden path. We ascended into a pine forest that unleashed a glorious aroma as the trees were warmed by the sun's first rays. It was perhaps already 9am, but the sun can take a while to reach you in the Himalaya. We re-joined the road for a while, which meandered up the side of the valley, but we soon forsook this route and made a bee-line for the top.

I passed an old man and greeted him with a *Namaste,* which caused his face to light up with a huge grin, and he responded with another *Namaste.* I passed two young school girls in identical uniforms apparently on their way to class. There was quite a steep drop into a ravine on one side, the other a vertical dirt wall. The path was less than 30cm wide. I stopped and moved to the edge to let them pass. They didn't bat an eye lid, but once past me, they both called out 'thank you' in unison, without even turning around. 'You're welcome,' I called, but they were already gone.

It was exhausting work climbing out of our first valley. My old man would call it 'a real lung-buster'. By the time we had reached the top, we had ascended only 300 vertical metres, but it was straight up.

We sat down for a rest.

'You know that me and the Nima was worried for you,' Subash said as we sat on green grass overlooking a gloriously sun-lit valley. There was barely a sound, save for a gust of wind blowing gently below us in the valley. A small twin engine plane soared overhead, bound for Lukla with a plane load of tourists. Cirrus clouds high above us formed an intriguing pattern in the sky. It made me feel abundantly happy. Here I was, sitting in the foothills of the Himalaya, and I had it all to myself. Save for a lone Canadian trekker marching the opposite way towards Jiri, I did not see one other foreigner on the hike to Shivalaya. Great for me, but not so great for the businesses that sit and watch potential income flying straight over their heads.

'Why was that?' I asked.

'Well this is a tough trek man, and we was worried how you going to go. We didn't know if your walking is good. But now I saw you walk and I am happy. I keep turning around and say *"Teksa? teksa?"* Asking if you is ok. And always you say, *"Teksa teksa."* This is good man. *Bistari bistari.* Slowly slowly. I tell you now man, best cure in Himalaya is water. If you is drinking four litres of water each day, no way you will get mountain sickness for sure.'

I felt pretty pleased with myself. We stood up and gently strolled across the ridge-line, covered in much of the same pine-trees as lower down in the valley. Something grand caught the corner of my left eye; the scale of which I knew was huge, despite not even knowing what it was. I turned my head slowly, and stood dumbstruck to see the largest mountains I have ever seen in my life. They were probably 50km away, but the size and majesty of them made them seem close enough to touch. You could see heavy snow gracing the peaks, of which we could see dozens, while glaciers carved their way down the slopes. Now it felt like we were in the Himalayas.

'What are those mountains, Subash?' I asked him.

'Those are not mountains, those are hills.' He shat on my parade.

*

Shivalaya, our destination for the night, sits at an altitude of 1767m (5797ft), so we had a good 600 metres to descend, and in true Himalayan spirit, it was pretty much straight down. We made our way into a steep gully being formed by the relentless flow of glacial melt water. Rhododendron flowers – the gorgeous national flower of Nepal, a brilliant red in colour, and large enough to cover the palm of your hand – were beginning to blossom, telling us that spring was about to be in full swing. The lower we went, the gentler the slope became, until we were walking almost horizontally next to a picturesque stream with miraculously clear water flowing quickly between perfectly rounded stones. We came across an iron suspension bridge and crossed it into Shivalaya. What a lovely little place it is.

A second suspension bridge brought us into the actual township, which was absolutely immaculate. There wasn't a single piece of rubbish on the ground, which was in stark contrast to Jiri, which was, if I'm honest, a bit of a tip. Immediately on the right Subash turned into the River Guest House, sat down, threw his arms out wide and said, 'Welcome to Shivalaya man, this is your second Himalayan home.'

The River Guest House was painted in exactly the same format as every other lodge in Shivalaya. It is painted in white and blue – the walls all being white and the railings blue – achieving quite a striking effect. Nima picked up my keys and hauled my bag up onto the next floor up and deposited it in my room. I climbed up the three widely-spaced stairs to get up onto the veranda and cautiously tip-toed my way across the floor made from unfastened wooden planks that flexed and groaned under my weight. It must have looked like I was walking the tight-rope, because I looked down to see Subash laughing so hard I was worried he was going to piss himself.

I ducked my way through a five-foot high doorway and into my second room. A three-quarter sized single bed lay up against the far wall, which was made of some kind of mortar, and painted a hideous shade of lime green. The other walls were made of wooden planks not altogether properly spaced, which left gaps at irregular intervals, giving key-whole glimpses of the adjacent rooms. The sound carried. You could hear a mouse fart in any one of those rooms. I prodded the bed gently and almost broke a fingernail.

'What do you want for lunch man?' Subash asked me as I re-joined the boys downstairs.

'Do they have Dal Bhat?'

'Of course man.'

Well, it was aromatic and the green vegetables were exceptionally flavoursome, however I think the actual lentil soup itself lacked a bit of a kick. The pickled vegetables were very spicy, but they lost marks on one of the side plates, serving this vegetable that I have never seen before that was sour enough to make your tongue shrivel up and die. It was inedible. It may have just been there for presentation.

After lunch Subash led me for a walk a little further down into the valley alongside the river. It was just a perfect setting for a town. The area looked like the mergence of three-or-so valleys and Shivalaya had plonked itself smack-bang in the middle of it. I can imagine the person, all those years ago, that strolled into this valley and thought: '*I want to live here.*' Why wouldn't ya?

Chapter Five

SHIVALAYA TO BHANDAR

Despite the circumstances I slept rather well in Shivalaya and by 7am I emerged from the lodge into beams of sunlight being shot out of an impossibly deep-blue sky. I raised both fists in the air, leant back, raised my face to the sky and did a tremendous Chewbacca yawn. Everywhere mothers ushered their children inside, windows closed, doors slammed shut and vacancy signs were turned around the other way.

I looked over to my left and saw an old man walking my way, crossing the suspension bridge in a slow, deliberate manner. He was carrying a large cardboard box. I pulled up a pew and watched him with interest. Then I watched in horror as he stopped half-way across, turned to the side of the bridge and unloaded the contents of the box straight down into that sublime-looking, crystal-clear water. It was his rubbish. My jaw dropped. If you'd done that where I'm from, you'd have been thrown in after it for the crocodiles' breakfast.

The night before, my isolation from other tourists had been brought to an end with the arrival of two Australian blokes in their late twenties named Dale and Andy, along with two Swedish trekkers. We'd sat up for a while in the communal area drinking a few beers and sharing notes on our respective trips. But mostly we just talked about squatting dunnies and our experiences of them.

We assembled in the courtyard at roughly the same time.

'Ok so Alex this morning is the first of the difficult,' Subash told me in what was to become an every-morning briefing. I noticed that the other four trekkers tuned in as well. 'We is going up for maybe the two hours, maybe one and the half hours, maybe the three hours. It is depending on you. *Bistari bistari,* slowly slowly we go and we is getting there quickly. We have lunch in Deurali, then we is going back down to the Bhandar to be sleeping. Any questions?'

'Nope, let's do it.'

I was a little bit apprehensive about this morning's trek. Yesterday had been a doddle in comparison, because this morning we had to go straight up for a vertical kilometre (3280ft) to Deurali, which sits at an altitude of 2705m (8874 ft).

We all hit the trail one after the other, with the two other Aussies in the lead, followed by myself and then the two Swedes. The climb was arduous. I'd take 15 to 20 steps, and pause for a minute to catch my breath before taking another 15 to 20 steps. This time there was no hiding my breathing. It is hard when you're gasping. After perhaps 10 minutes of climbing I allowed myself a little break and a drink of water. I turned around and was shocked to see that the rusting, corrugated iron rooves of Shivalaya's 40-or-so buildings were already a distant speck. Perhaps I wasn't making such bad time.

I remounted my pack and kept going. It wasn't long before I rounded up Dale and Andy and overtook them when the path was wide enough for me to do so. I complemented myself on choosing to bring a porter along with me (those guys had a guide, Gopal, but were sharing a porter, forcing them to carry a lot of their own stuff in different packs, while the Swedes were completely on their own). Before too long I was out of sight. Although I am a competitive person, I knew it wasn't a race and that we were trekking for the love of being out in the wilderness and to see the greatest mountain range of them all; but once I overtook those guys, I refused to let them catch me again. I had a lot of fitness to gain for the passes, so I knew a bit of imaginary competition would be good for me.

A couple of hours passed. Large, nameless and snow-graced mountains appeared behind, giving me a legitimate excuse to stop, breathe and snap some photographs.

At 10.10am I dragged my knackered ass over a rocky staircase and realised with the most wondrous feeling of elation that I could climb no higher. We had arrived at Deurali, announced by a multitude of prayer flags strewn from anything you could possibly tie a piece of string to, as well as several rocky walls that ran the length of the town with a seemingly infinite number of Buddhist incantations carved into the surface.

'Please, sit down,' said Subash while turning around to face me, but unbeknownst to him, I already was. A smile, followed by a look that may have been pity overcame his face. Then he added, 'Wait here, I get us some things.'

I sat there in the sunlight, recovering, ever so happy that we only had to go down for the rest of the day. I watched with interest – or at least that's what I'm going to call it – as Subash returned from a little shop carrying two glasses of what looked to be urine with a little steam coming off the top. I let out a moan while he was still out of earshot, dreading a hot drink when all I could think about was an ice-cold refreshment.

'Here man I get this for us,' he said.

'What is it?'

'Just drink it man.'

I didn't like the sound of this. If he couldn't even tell me what it was, that meant it was not a good thing. I had a sip, and my face tried to implode into the back of my skull. It was the most sour, revolting thing I have ever tasted in my life. Take the most disgusting white wine you've ever tried, pee in it a little bit, and you would not even be close to experiencing what I did that day (but it would be a good start).

'How is it man?' he asked.

I had another sip.

'It's good,' I said, although my voice had taken on the sound of a man who had smoked two packs a day for the last 80 years.

'It is alcohol?'

'Yes it is a Rakshi. It is the local wine.'

'Man it's not even eleven o'clock.'

'You no want it?' he asked, a little hurt.

'Yes I want it,' I replied, going into diplomat mode. 'Sorry man, just not used to drinking alcohol at ten thirty in the morning. But it's ok, I'm on holiday.'

He seemed pleased with my response, and the smile returned to his face. Having shot myself in the foot, I now had to finish the wine. I waited until he wasn't looking, readied a snickers bar, pinched my nose and skulled the cat piss, then shoved a snickers in my mouth and chewed violently, before releasing the grip I had on my nostrils. It had soured – nay, ruined – my Snickers bar, but the alternative still keeps me up at night.

*

As it turns out, Rakshi is stronger than an ox, and I was forced into a light-headed descent into Bhandar. We approached the other side of the town (it was barely 50 metres long) and looked straight down. We could see our target at the bottom of our next valley. Bhandar lies at an altitude of 2200m, so we had a good 500 vertical metres to descend.

We made our way down an excellent trekker path, made of large stones piled constructively to form a kind of staircase. The distant and daunting Lamjura Pass slipped in and out of view as we dropped into a dry, desolate valley. It didn't take too long, the stroll to Bhandar. Nima had gone ahead with the bags and as I rounded a bend I saw him sitting on a large rock, waiting for us to catch up. He had Nepali music blaring from his phone. I smiled and took a seat next to him and just kind of breathed it all in.

It was dry, but beautiful in a different way, this valley. We continued before too long, leaving the rocky staircase above us, moving on to the gently undulating valley floor. Then suddenly we were in Bhandar and it was only 2pm. Subash checked me in at the Shobha Lodge and Restaurant, a cream-coloured, three-storey building made from mortar, with all the doors and window frames painted a deep, forest-green colour. Tradition dictated that I treat myself to an Everest Beer, so that's exactly what I did.

Chapter Six

Bhandar to Sete and over the Lamjura Pass

We all left Bhandar at the same time, but it wasn't long before the Swedes dropped out of sight. The path ran horizontal for a good long while, much to my delight, with only the slightest of elevation changes. After a while the path narrowed and we could peer over the edge and see a drop of perhaps a thousand feet down to a river that thundered violently below us. I watched in interest as two figures made their way slowly down a path. I squinted against the sunlight and realised that it was, in fact, our two Swedish friends.

'Subash, look, it's those Swedish guys!' I called to him.

'Ah yes, they is taking the old ways,' he answered me. 'This is the very long ways, maybe is adding them two hours onto the trekking.'

'The guides just paid for themselves,' said Dale in the dramatic voice of an American movie trailer narrator.

We began losing altitude as we dropped down towards a quaint little town called Kinja, which at 1630m (5347ft), was the lowest point of my entire trek. We pulled in for lunch, sitting in the sunlight and watching as hybrid yaks made their way through the town, carrying supplies to restock the mountain shops and lodges. We'd eaten lunch, rested, filled up water bottles and were about to leave when a pair of tired looking Swedes scrambled into town with very confused looks on their faces.

*

I had a tough afternoon. The path zigzagged its way up the face of a very steep valley wall. It was real agricultural country. At times, huge buffalos blocked the path and we warily had to circumnavigate them without falling off the track. Everywhere rhododendron flowers added some much needed colour to the dry, brown countryside. Up and up we continued to go. Honestly, it wasn't a lot of fun. It was warm, I was leaking from every pore, my tired legs were aching from the previous day's toil and we still had a long way to go. At 2520 metres (8267ft), Sete was a good 900 metres higher than Kinja, and it was an entire backflip from the previous days, when we'd completed all the climbing in the morning. Now we had a hard slog straight after lunch after a very easy morning.

Whose stupid fucking idea was this? I berated myself. *Yay, let's go 'walking' in the Himalayan foothills.*

Anyway, I shan't complain. I passed a family sitting on the ground. Mum, dad and four kids, and they were just there having the best time in each other's company. They laughed, sang and called out a heart-warming 'namaste' to me as I trundled on past them. They lightened my mood considerably. Once high above them and out of sight, I asked Subash if it would be alright to take a photo of them. He said it wasn't a problem, so I put on my largest lens and snapped a picture that I just love to look at.

The house was built on a steep slope, so although they were sitting on the ground, they were actually at roof height. The roof itself consisted of wooden slats being held down by large rocks, while the walls were just shaped stones piled on top of each other, but were not held together by any kind of slurry. Woven straw was spread at intervals to aid in the waterproofing process. How effective it actually was, I'm not sure.

In a better mood, I made my way into Sete, checking in at the rather grand-looking Sunrise Lodge and Restaurant, made of carved stone and corrugated iron. The first thing I always did when going in to a new lodge for the first time was to check the toilet. My jaw dropped when I saw a western-style dunny in this place. *Hooray!*

My room was small, but had a double bed in it, a rare luxury. I think if I'd thrown the mattress on the floor and slept on the rungs, it may have been slightly more comfortable. The walls were made of spaced pine that was taped together to prevent other people from seeing in. When they had run out of tape, they had simply stuffed cloth or linen in between the gaps.

A thunderous noise in the night wrenched me instantly from a deep slumber. It was pitch-black, but I could feel things landing on my sleeping bag. I fumbled around blindly for my head torch, and shivering I managed to flick the light on. Well, it was hailing. And it was hailing inside my room. I sighed a deep and heart-felt sigh and watched as ice particles landed all around me. I flicked the light off, crawled deeper into my sleeping bag, pulled the cord tight above my head, and cocooned myself off from the world.

*

The new day dawned miraculously bright. The air was cool and clearer than crystal. Birds chirped and flowers blossomed. I was a touch apprehensive this day. It was Lamjura Pass day. The guide book told me to eat well this morning, so I ordered two of everything; two omelettes, two pieces of Tibetan Bread (kind of a mixture of white bread and a doughnut) and a large pot of masala chai tea. Subash looked at me as though I had gone mad, but I finished it all, packed my stuff and waddled out through the front door.

'Ok Alex,' Subash began, and I knew I was about to get a briefing for the day.

'Why does he call you Alex?' Dale interrupted.

'Yeah I don't know. You know my name is Gordon, right Subash?'

'Yes, but is the very hard name to be saying,' He defended himself.

'I don't know why, you have every single one of those letters in your alphabet.'

'Ok, so you no want me to call you Mr Alex?'

'Well, I don't really care, but it just isn't my name.'

'Ok so Mr Gorong, today we are doing the Lamjura Pass,' said Subash, continuing his briefing. Dale and I looked at each other and began laughing, but Subash continued undeterred. 'Is the pass at 3530 metres. If you can't do this pass, there is no ways you can do the Three Passes trekking. So take your time, carry your jacket because weather maybe bad at the pass, and let's go.'

Off we went for perhaps 20 metres of level ground before the ascent really began. It is hard to describe the trail better than it's described in *Lonely Planet: Trekking in the Nepal Himalaya*, which says, 'The trail picks its way through a dripping, moss-cloaked forest of gnarled rhododendron, magnolia, maple and birch trees.'

It wasn't long before we reached the snowline, pushing on for hour after hour towards the cloudless sky. We clambered over large roots that disrupted the path, pushed branches out of our way, fought our way over mossy rocks and leapt lightly over fallen trees. Despite the exertion required, I was having quite a good time. Dale and Andy were going for it this morning and I found it hard to match their blistering pace, so I just went at my own speed and continued to enjoy myself.

We stopped for a rest and a lemon and ginger tea at a small shop which offered the most amazing views of Mount Numbur's pyramidal peak. The Sherpa name for the mountain is Shorong Yul Lha, meaning 'God of the Solu'. Standing at 6959 metres (22831ft), it was the tallest mountain I had ever seen.

Clouds began to form above the pass and the wind picked up. The temperature plummeted and despite the heat my body was generating from the climb, I was forced to pull my jacket on. As lunch time approached, so too did the pass; and as I took my final, weary steps towards the restaurant we would be eating at, I saw a little boy of perhaps only three years in my peripheral vision with a snowball in his hand. I looked at him and smiled. He smiled back and went to throw the snowball at me, but it landed about a didgeridoo's length from him, and absolutely nowhere near me. I laughed and made my own snowball and did a little underarm throw which broke gently on his jacket, to his utter delight. I went closer to him and allowed him to hit me with the next snowball. I looked up to see his mother watching us from the doorway, laughing with joy that her son had found someone to play with.

It was getting cold and it began to snow ever so gently, almost imperceptible to the human eye. I needed to get inside and thaw out my frozen hands. Inside I found the gang in a small room, seated in a semi-circle around an old, clay oven. Subash barked an order and Nima jumped up to give me his seat, right in front of the oven. I put my hand on his shoulder and insisted that he keep his seat, which made him feel a little uneasy, but he soon overcame this and was his happy self once more.

We all sat and watched as the lady of the house prepared the food right in front of us. Having a love for all things cooking, I felt deeply privileged to witness this spectacle unfold, and I made a great deal of mental notes on all the ingredients and techniques that she applied to achieve some really delicate flavours. When I returned to Australia nearly a month later, I missed Dhal Bhat Takheri, and so I began making it for myself, based largely on what I had seen this lady do on a little yak-dung stove at the top of a high pass.

Outside Andy asked a middle-aged woman for permission to give her son a small piece of candy. He was about two years old, as cute as a button and had snot sprawled up either side of his face. He took the sweet and then looked at his mother, who said something like, '*Now what do you say*?'

He put his hands together, lifted them up to just below his chin in a praying action, and bowed his head slightly while muttering some form of 'thank you'. It was just too cute. Then I looked down, and this little newborn puppy with the bushiest mountain hair came stumbling towards me and chirped – it wasn't a bark - and I just couldn't believe all the cuteness. I really couldn't. I threw on my backpack, snapped a quick photo of the cute dog, cried out '*zam zam!*', and we were off like a dog shot in the arse.

We went over a final rise that marked the pass, snapped some pictures of the cairn and prayer flag, before dropping down into yet another valley. It is quite a strange sensation. For two days we'd been making our way along the floor of the last valley, and that view was all we had. It was spectacular, don't get me wrong, but it is your whole world. Then, within seconds of going over the pass, you no longer have the view you had before, but are instead presented with a whole new view; and it will be your entire world until you scramble into the next valley. This world we entered now was prehistoric.

Ancient fir and rhododendron trees formed a dense forest that stifled the path. Some of the trees soared at least 50 metres or more from the ground and it seriously looked like a scene from *Jurassic Park*. The descent was gradual over loose football-sized rocks, so you could never take your eyes from your feet for too long. We walked for perhaps two hours before the track took a steeper approach and we dropped dramatically into the little township of Junbesi. Most people stay in Junbesi for the night as most guide books for the area recommend this, but Subash had a different idea. He persuaded me to carry on past Junbesi to stay at the Everest View Hotel, where (you guessed it) I should be able to get my first view of Everest the following morning.

'Subash, I'm really tired mate, how far is this hotel?' I asked while plonking myself on the ground.

'Is only a gradual climb, maybe one and half hours.'

'Ok,' I sighed, getting back to my feet and walking out of Junbesi. We crossed a wooden bridge over a raging river and I followed Subash to the base of a hill that he began to climb.

'Hold on, hold on.' I stopped him. 'We are going up there?'

'Yes man.'

If I stood at the base of the slope with toes touching the bottom, I could almost touch the wall at head-height with an outstretched arm. I don't care where you're from, that is not a gradual climb.

'Subash, that is not gradual mate, that is a fucking cliff!'

'Yes but peoples in Nepal are calling this the flat country. We is calling it 'the Nepali Flat'.'

'I'll flatten you,' I grumbled under my breath. Sulking, I joined him on the precipice and willed my exhausted legs to keep pushing me up. The rest of the day was a blur. I was utterly spent. I plundered on in a bubble of pain and anguish. *It better be clear tomorrow,* I thought.

Eventually we stumbled upon the hotel.

'I'll have one beer and two waters!' I cried as I struggled over the final (and always incredibly steep) few stairs.

I was the last to arrive, so naturally I was shunted in to the worst room in the house. The bed was so short that my knees dangled over the edge. The mattress seemed to be made of sheeted titanium and it was so uncomfortable that my mind refused to enter a subconscious state, despite my utter fatigue. So I just kind of laid there, not daring to move in case I exposed any inch of skin to the cold, cold air, as visions of mountains drifted through my tired mind.

Chapter Seven

GLIMPSING EVEREST AND GETTING SICK

I was up with the first light and dressed quickly. We were at 2900 metres (9514 ft) above sea level and the mornings saw temperatures plummet to well below freezing. I made my way eagerly over to a viewing platform and just stared at the stage in front of me. Everest was off to the left of the picture and was about the size of my thumbnail.

It was hard to feel any emotional attachment to something so far away. To something that I had come from so far away to see. The looming peaks in the forefront of the view seemed so much higher than us, but were in fact over 2km lower. These 6000-something metre peaks were gorgeous, knife-edged ridges rising almost vertically up into a crystal clear sky. And then there was Everest, a thick black chunk, unable to boast any kind of eloquence. It looked like the ugly duckling that had been shunted to the back of the picture. But then the sun glinted over a distant mountain, the barrier to the valley, and Everest caught the golden reflection in the plume of snow being wind-blasted from the summit. Everest alone had a snow plume, so Everest alone glistened in gold. I stood and stared for what felt like an eternity, my eyes transfixed on the summit, the highest point on earth.

I ate breakfast with the Sherpas in the kitchen - another omelette with Tibetan bread – before getting the hell out of that place. It was a real shit pit.

We passed a little girl in the morning that stopped me to ask something in the Nepalese language.

'What did she say, Subash?'

'She wants you to give her a balloon.'

I laughed, thinking it was rather random. I instead gave her a Mars Bar and she seemed pretty content with that.

It was quite an uneventful day. Other than seeing a pair of monkeys and hundreds and hundreds of mules, nothing really interesting happened. My knees began to ache from the pressure exerted on them after all the descending we had done over the past few days; but the other guide, Gopal, was also complaining of sore knees, so I guessed it was just normal.

The final trek took us down through to the town of Nanthala, and then it was a casual stroll through a cosy looking town to the Himalayan Trekker Lodge. It was always the most amazing feeling arriving at your lodge for the night. Then you'd get busy with some hiker rituals. Once you arrive at your lodge you don't have to be anywhere or do anything. It is marvellous. So I'd savour the sensation of taking my boots off, allowing myself a good 10 to 15 minutes to slowly remove them. I'd seen a sign advertising a hot-water shower. So I informed the man of my intention, he added $4 to my bill, and then I went into the shower room. It had been five days since I had showered and I had climbed about 5500 vertical metres (18000ft) in that time. I was a bit stinky.

I'm not going to say it was glorious. The water came out in more of a mist than a stream. It took about 10 minutes for the water to heat up, which left me standing in the middle of a freezing cold room, butt naked, wondering why on earth I hadn't run the shower before undressing. It took about five minutes to get sufficiently wet enough to even form a lather with the soap, and then about 20 minutes to get it all washed off. And I was shivering the whole time. I managed to get dressed and shivered my way up to my sleeping bag, but realised as I entered my room that my backpack, and therefore my sleeping bag, still had not arrived. Where was Nima? I quickly jumped back into the filthy clothes I'd been wearing all day, notified Subash of Nima's absence, then crawled into bed (apparently made from diamond, but without the beauty) and covered myself with a paper-thin blanket.

I lay there, shivering and unable to move for three hours, before a very drunk Nima stumbled into my room and laughed while he apologised. I frowned at him, grabbed my sleeping bag, and in one swift movement I was inside, instantly warmer. Nima stammered something that made no sense, walked into my wall and almost fell over, and fumbled for the door handle before finally exiting the room. I heard him clatter his way down the stairs. Subash came in two minutes later to apologise profusely on his behalf.

*

I woke up in Nunthala with a terrible pain in my stomach, and I knew immediately that something was wrong. I had diarrhoea. Worse than that, I had severe food poisoning. I went to the toilet three times before I was able to leave the guesthouse that morning, and the whole travelling group had already left by the time I was ready. I stumbled across everyone, having a break after about one hour.

'Ah you are behind us, we thought you must have left early this morning,' Said Andy as he saw me round the corner.

'Nah I was on the dunny,' I said.

'What did he just say?' A Canadian man that I had never seen before asked.

'Oh dunny,' Replied Dale. 'It means toilet. We have our own language.'

After a good several-hour slog, we pulled into a small village for lunch, but food was the last thing on my mind. Subash, however, forced me to order a bowl of vegetable noodle soup to keep my strength up. I was half way through it and had to stop. I needed the dunny again.

I could see Bupsa, our destination for the night, suspended high up on a mountain ledge, way, way above us. It was a daunting prospect.

'Come on *zam zam!*' I said to Subash, as I just wanted to get going.

We walked for about 35 seconds - we weren't even out of the same village yet - before a massive stomach gripe had me doubled over in pain. Subash noticed and called over to a woman sitting on a rock ledge by the side of the trail, who pointed down a dark, narrow alleyway between two old-looking, moss-covered stone buildings. I waited while Subash went to investigate. He returned moments later and waved me in. What greeted me was pretty disgusting. Pretty horrific actually, but it didn't matter, I needed to go.

Ten minutes later I was sitting outside near the woman on the trail, sweat dripping from my forehead. I reluctantly sipped on my bottle of water that I knew would terrorise my stomach in minutes. There was nothing for it, I had to keep moving. It seemed like hours went by as we climbed up to Bupsa. The path was rocky; sometimes loose, sometimes fixed, sometimes breath-takingly steep, and at other times gently climbing, but never did we go downhill. The gripes started almost immediately after setting off, but there was simply nowhere to go. On one side there was a terraced field of barley, and on the uphill side a farrow, steep incline exposed to the track that snaked upwards.

It seemed like the climb took hours, but eventually Bupsa became visible as we rounded a rock buttress. There were a few nervous moments coming into the town, but I was soon reunited with the toilet.

I did a whole lot of nothing in Bupsa. I had managed to secure the room right next to the toilet. I laid in bed at 3pm that afternoon, and didn't get out of it until 8am the next morning. I ate and drank nothing, giving my stomach no fuel to add to the fire. I laid there in the afternoon, while it was still light, and gazed out the window. I wasn't lonely, but content, just staring and staring at the world that was so foreign to mine. A crow flew into view and circled above the guest house a few times, before sitting right on top of a large spindly pine tree, as though he were the angel on top of a Christmas tree.

The dark green of the pine and the black of the crow set against a perfect ocean-blue sky would have made an excellent photo. I looked at my camera bag. It was within an arm's reach. I looked back at the crow, and watched for a few minutes more. I barely had the strength to move. I closed my eyes for a few minutes. *If he is still there when I open my eyes, I'll get a photo of him,* I thought to myself. I opened them slowly. The crow was still there, but I was still too weak to move.

'Excuse me very much, excuse me very much Mr Alex.' I heard Subash at the door, awakening me from my slumber. 'Morning man, how many times you went to the toilet last night?'

'None man, but probably only because I haven't eaten since those noodles yesterday for lunch.'

'This is a very good thing man,' he said, enthused.

'I don't think so mate.'

'What you is wanting for your breakfast?'

I made a noise of utter disgust and looked away.

'You must be eating some things man,' he insisted.

'Alright bring me a packet of dried noodles and a snickers bar for later.'

We left Bupsa after I had forced down some noodles and water. It didn't take long before the stomach noises began and I was once again forced to stop. The path began as it had left off the day before, climbing up gradually until it reached the pass. I became fatigued beyond belief. After about an hour of climbing, I was literally climbing for 20 metres before needing a break. Progress was tediously slow. By the time I reached the top, it was lunch time, and I was a spent force. Every step was agony.

We rounded a bend just below the pass and took in a glorious view up the valley with interlocking spurs stabbing down a few degrees from vertical, culminating in the epic frame of Cho Oyu on the distant horizon. I was beginning to feel incredibly ill. Way down below I could see a few settlements speckled at intervals along the trail.

'I'm not going to make Khare,' I said to Subash.

'I know man,' he replied. 'I think maybe today you should have rested.'

No shit.

We now entered the most dangerous part of the trek between Jiri and Lukla. It was a steep descent on a trail that was muddy and scattered with loose stones. Often the mud in the middle of the trail was so deep that it was necessary to walk right on the edge above a drop to unknown depths, on stones that looked like they *wanted* to throw you off the trail. Often we shared the trail with mules and hybrid yaks that cared not one bit for our safety.

As I began descending, my condition deteriorated rapidly. My head became light and I felt dizzy. My legs began to feel as though they didn't belong to me. It wasn't ideal given the state of the path. I plodded on, out of breath, even though we were going down-hill, getting dizzier and dizzier as the hours rolled on. Cruelly, Puiyan, our destination, dangled itself right there in front of us like bait on a hook. But it's hard to gauge scale in the Himalayas, and Puiyan was a long way away. We came across a group of porters huddled around having a chat, and I just kind of slumped down beside them on a rock. I think I sat there for a long time, but I'm not sure. Their voices, although right next to me, sounded like they were a million miles away. We were sitting right next to a waterfall, but it seemed to make no sound. After a time, Subash summoned me to my feet and we walked slowly on.

Subash was an expert at staying out of the mud. His boots were lined with probably one millimetre of mud up the sides, as were every other local's on the trail. I had long since given up on agility and with my lack of control my boots were completely submersed in mud. The inside of my trousers all the way up to my knees were covered in mud and mule shit. I hadn't the strength to care. I knew everyone I passed was talking about me. The Nepalese have no shame in talking about you to your face, especially when you don't understand their language. In fact, you can catch them when they think they are being subtle just by bursting out laughing when they do. I did that a few times and received some mortified looks in return.

Eventually I reached a stage of utter exhaustion. My head felt like I had devoured half a bottle of rum in seconds. I felt drunk, but not in a good way. We crossed a metal bridge and then I sat down at the foot of the town. I was almost there, but I wasn't moving for the next 15 minutes. Then we secured a room at the Beehive Lodge, which was a brick-like cottage set-up.

'I have to go look for Nima,' Subash said.

'You don't think he will come?'

'Maybe coming, maybe no. Like yesterday long time coming. And I worries man, because he saw his friend up there and maybe drinking.'

'Ok,' I said, and immediately fell into a deep sleep. I don't think he had even left the room.

I awoke at 5pm – I had been out for about two hours – to the sight of Subash carrying my backpack into the room.

'Did you find Nima?' I asked, a little dazed and confused.

'Yes found him. Nima is a drunk. I find him all the ways back at the beginning of paths. When he sees me he is a very scared.'

'Ah, again. Can you pass me my sleeping bag please?'

I was freezing cold and I had started to shiver without my clothes. Two days in a row. Nima was in the bad books.

'Come man, you must eat something.'

'Just give me 10 minutes,' I said, needing to warm up before going outside.

I soon joined him in what would have been a pleasant courtyard had I not been in such a state. I sat down and together we watched the path from where we had come, looking for any signs of a bag-less Nima. I ordered dinner (I think it was some kind of potato dish) and a cup of ginger tea.

*

'Can you please bring my dinner to the room man?' I asked. 'I need to go lay down.'

I was suddenly overcome with a wave of sickness. I stood, and took a step away from the bench I was sitting on. It felt like the blood in my feet began to boil, before the sensation shot upwards towards my head. I had taken probably six or eight steps towards my room, when my head was overwhelmed by the sensation. I remember falling. I had fainted.

I was out for a matter of seconds, as Subash, who was sprinting towards me, had not yet made it to me.

'Are you okay man, are you okay?' He asked with a very worried look of his face.

'Not really.' I remember saying as nausea took control of my brain.

Subash grabbed my hands and started to rub them furiously with his, as though this were some kind of Nepali cure for fainting. I sat on the ground for a long time.

'I can't believe I just fainted.' I said, realising it was even weirder that I could remember the whole thing, from the sensation in my head, to hitting the deck. I must have realised I was going down, because I landed

95

with arms outstretched, as if to protect myself. I was remarkably unharmed seeing as I fell into a kind of drain, slightly lower than the surface of the courtyard.

At long last the nausea passed. Subash helped me to my feet, but instantly the same, sickening feeling engulfed me, and I fell forward, this time onto the table, but again with outstretched arms that somehow managed to support my body weight. I lowered my head onto the table, still standing, and shut my eyes. If that table had not have been there, I would have fainted twice. I felt strong arms grab me and guide me onto the stone steps where I sat with a thud.

Sitting up I still felt sick. So I laid down on my back, eyes closed, and willed that god-awful feeling away. I opened my eyes and Subash had opened a Snickers bar, broken off half of it, and was trying to force feed me.

'Eat!' He demanded.

I did eat. And I did feel better.

'You not eaten anything in two days man!' He said. 'How you going to walks in the Himalaya like that? Maybe we should be flying back into the Kathmandu. You have insurance, I know this. I have your insurance papers. Maybe we get the helicopters back to the Kathmandu.'

I shook my head, unable to formulate words, I was in a bit of shock. I can't recall ever fainting in my life. Before I had fainted I was really cold and looking forward to getting back into my sleeping bag. Now I was dripping with sweat and boiling hot. The cold air actually felt revitalising on my skin. The next thing I knew I was in bed and a plate of potatoes cooked in turmeric had been shoved in front of me.

Chapter Eight

JOINING THE KHUMBU HIGHWAY

I had severe stomach cramps all night and needed to use the facilities on three separate occasions. You don't realise the ordeal until you need to get out of bed, get layered up, find your head torch in the utter blackness of night, put on your boots, leave the room and walk to the communal toilet, squat down and try not to squirt on your clothes, before doing it all in the reverse order once back in your room. Repeat that a few times in the night in a weakened state and you'll end up frustrated, I assure you.

As the morning light began peaking in through little holes in the door, my eyes opened and I stared at the ceiling. All things considered, I didn't feel too bad. A gentle knock at the door announced the arrival of Subash.

'Excuse me very much, excuse me very much, Mr. Gorong.' I heard him call. 'May I come in?'

'Come in.' I called to him, having deliberately left the door unlocked for this very reason.

'Mr Gorong, how are you?'

'I think I'm ok.'

'Maybe we should be having the rest day, like in the Bupsa when we didn't be having the rest day.'

'No way mate. I am sick of the sight of this room.' I replied using some kind of an idiom.

'You is sick, so we should be having the rest day.'

'No, it's a saying. It means I don't want to see this room ever again!'

'Ok so if you can eat some things, we will go slowly to Khare.'

'Ok mate, I'll have two pieces of dried toast.'

'Ok so two pieces of toast, some Tibetan bread and an omelette.' He negotiated.

I laughed for the first time in days.

'I'll meet you half way. I'll have toast and the Tibetan bread.'

'Ah, the Nima has come.' Said Subash who was looking over his shoulder to the courtyard. We watched as he approached the room, eyes firmly fixed on the floor and pushed opened the door a little wider to enter my room. I was still lying in bed, watching him. He shuffled ever so slowly into the room, which instantly took on the aroma of a brewery. Then, quick-as-a-flash, he covered the distance between himself and me, grabbed my hand, dropped to his knees and began pressing my hand to his forehead.

'So a sorry sah, so a sorry sah, so a sorry sah.' He said repeatedly for over a minute as I watched in interest. After a time, I put my other hand on his shoulder and asked him to stop. He looked at me with blood-shot puppy-dog eyes.

'Nima, don't do that again ok. I was very sick.'

'So a sorry sah, so a sorry sah.'

'It's ok, just never again, ok?'

A small smile returned to his face and he jumped up and began frantically packing my things for me into my backpack. When he finished he left the room without a backward glance.

'The Nima thought you would be a firing him.' Subash said in a matter-of-fact kind of way. 'If he is losing his job, maybe his family won't be eating, so very important the Nima is keeping this job.'

'Well the Nima better not get drunk and not show up again.'

'He won't be doing this again, trust me.'

*

I ate the breakfast and waited anxiously for a backlash, but to my astonishment it never eventuated. We walked along level ground for a time, 'a little bit up and a little bit down', as Subash would say. A black dog came running around the corner, spotted us, then just sat down on the path and waited for us. He was typically hairy and very wise-looking. As we approached he turned around 180 degrees and walked with us for a short while, and then satisfied we knew the way, he let out a single bark, announcing his intention to part ways, turned around and continued on his original path. It was bizarre.

The descent to Khare took three hours and it was all down. We checked into the first lodge we came across, even though it wasn't even midday. It was a sunny afternoon and we decided to relax in the garden, sitting with four Sherpa women that ran the lodge. An elderly lady sat there, holding a Buddhist necklace in her right hand, while constantly chanting the mantra, '*Om Mani Pädme Hum'*, over and over again, for hour after hour. I was enthralled by her dedication, but wondered if perhaps she hadn't slightly lost the plot. I took a little wander around the lodge and saw some of my clothes that had been filthy from the mule shit day, were sparkling clean and hanging from a makeshift clothesline.

'This is the Nima saying sorry.' Said Subash.

We went inside where there was a television about the size of a microwave that looked like it was one of the first ever invented. It projected a grainy picture of some Nepalese people prancing around a field and singing in the most ear-piercing of voices.

'What is this bloody song about Subash?' I asked him, realising he was singing along too.

'What all Nepali songs are about man.' He answered as if it were the most obvious thing in the world. 'It is about love.'

'It sounds like someone is dying.'

Suddenly the channel changed and I breathed a sigh of relief. A small boy, with the attention span of a newt, was in charge of the remote control. Suddenly the channel changed again. Then again. My god, he was a flicker. I bloody hate a flicker. He would be watching something, would burst out laughing, and then mid-laughter he would flick the channel. Surely that amount of raucous laughter at least deserved a few more minutes on that channel. I wanted to reach over, snatch the remote and donk him on the head with it.

*

The next day brought us to Monday the 10th of March and it was time we busted a move. I woke up at 4am with the realisation that I needed the toilet. Everyone has suffered from diarrhoea, I'm sure, so you will understand the post-traumatic stress that is involved every time you need the loo afterwards. So it was with some form of apprehension that I closed the distance between me and the hole in the floor. I needn't have worried.

Five minutes later I was back in my room, doing a happy dance, and, being mindful there were other guests the other side of paper-thin walls, I began to mime Ashford and Simpson's tune, *Solid as a Rock*!

I needed a change from Tibetan bread for breakfast, so I went with the porridge and apple option. I'm sorry for talking about toilets and bodily functions so much, I really am, but it was a huge part of my day-to-day existence. I'll cut this one short though. Nepali porridge with dried apples gives you a Himalayan amount of wind. Not exactly what you want when you're still in the post traumatic, not-really-sure-what-is-coming-out-of-your-bum stage. Enough said.

We left the guest house a little after 8am, and immediately began a steep climb up rocky stairs. It went on for a good few minutes and by the time I'd reached the top I was dripping with sweat, but absolutely loving it.

'I feel born again!' I said to Subash as we took the highest point in our stride. We then began a small descent by lightly tip-toeing over a gently flowing stream.

'Really? You is feeling like a this?' he asked.

'Yeah mate, I feel awesome.'

Not only had the taking-it-easy approach for two days cured my illness, but it had given my tired legs a chance to recuperate. I was powering up slopes and attacking hills with a vengeance before I realised I might be overdoing it. And so I slowed my pace a fraction. It is amazing what happens to the body once it becomes accustomed to climbing up and down all day, every day. You kind of plod up the steeper slopes in a rhythmic motion, always moving, but conserving energy. Yet when you come to a lesser incline, you can actually manage to turn it into a rest. Looking back on the first few days of the trek, this was not even remotely a possibility. Up was up, and that was the end of it. We climbed up for about an hour before the path levelled off and we came across a decent-sized place called Chheplung.

'Here the path from Lukla is joining,' Subash said.

I braced myself. I have been reading about the Khumbu region of Nepal for close to a decade, and if there's one thing that everyone makes abundantly clear, it's that the path from Lukla to Everest Base Camp is crowded. I was expecting London's M80 rat race at rush hour. I grimaced and stepped onto the new path. I opened my eyes, blinked a few times, looked around and realised I was the only tourist in sight.

'I reckon you blokes are at least half full of shit,' I said to Subash.

'What it means?'

'You tell me here too much busy, but all I can see is you and a yak.'

'No problems man. In Namche you see.'

'This is like when you tell someone a movie is going to be rubbish, but they watch it anyway, and it seems great because they are having a low expectation,' I explained slowly, making sure he was following me.

'What you mean man?'

'I mean that everyone told me this was going to be too busy, so I formed that idea in my head, so now it seems empty.'

'Yes I get it man. Very good.'

'Yes very good.'

We crossed a massive steel suspension bridge at least a hundred metres long before we began a gradual descent over unbelievably easy terrain. After crossing the Lamjura Pass, this seemed like a stroll in the woods.

'You are feeling hungry man?'

'No not really,' I answered. 'I can wait until Phakding for lunch.'

'Man we is already in the Phakding.'

I looked up. *So we were.* This was our destination for the night and it was only 11.30am. I wanted to keep going, but common sense prevailed. I'd only felt better for about 12 hours, so a nice easy day seemed like a good idea. We would be in Namche Bazaar the next day and it was supposed to feel like Las Vegas compared with where we had been.

I checked into the guest house called Beer Garden Lodge. It didn't have a beer garden, but it was absolutely huge. I was somehow shunted up to the third floor, and the steps to get there were steeper than anything I'd encountered on the trail that day. I had a look around, as per usual. I saw a mirror in the hallway. I started making noises like *ooooh* and *ahhhh*. Everything about this place was on a different scale compared to the poor lodges between Jiri and Lukla. I looked into the mirror, the first time I had seen my own face in 9 days, and recoiled in horror. Well not really, but my nose was incredibly dry and shedding everywhere. I snuck over to the bathroom (I felt like I was snooping around someone else's house), stuck my head in and had a look. I closed the door. I made my hands into fists and raised them both straight above my head in triumph. I would not be squatting tonight.

*

I had a good old lazy time in Phakding. I dined on spaghetti with tomato sauce for both lunch and dinner. The thought of rice or noodles made my stomach churn, so I turned to the Italians for solace. I casually strolled up and down the town in very light rain. It was refreshing. This was the flattest township I'd seen yet on my travels in this Himalayan kingdom. Subash and I explored the lodge, walking around its many levels. It was like a big wooden castle without the turrets or beer garden. We wandered around the back of the place where there were extensive vegetable patches. A couple of young boys were out picking the spinach and what looked to be some kind of Chinese vegetable in preparation for dinner tonight.

'See that?' asked Subash, pointing to a dead-looking mound of shrubs.

'Yep.'

'This is the marijuana tree,' he said.

'What's it doing there?'

'It is a growing naturally here. But maybe the owners no like it, so they kills it and leave there. Maybe also so not possible to get in trouble with the police.'

'That's unbelievable, that would be worth a fortune in my country,' I said.

We strolled back into the dining room, ordered a couple of lemon and ginger teas and sat drinking them in silence while listening to the various languages echoing across the large wooden hall. A rather obnoxious Australian woman grabbed a plastic chair, moved it over to the large steel oven that doubled as the room's heating, and put her hands over it mockingly as if to say to the staff, 'Why the bloody hell isn't this fire going?' It was, you understand, about 30°C in that room. Large glass windows lined the entire perimeter of the rectangular building, and early afternoon sunshine was streaming in, sending dust particles into a frenzy. I'm from the tropics and I was toasty.

Then her even more obnoxious husband came in. He was about 50 years old, and was obviously one of those bastards that liked to speak so that everyone could hear what he was saying; deliberately, as if he were the Dalai Lama or the Pope. Then he got out his laptop and started playing 2014 chart-smashing pop songs by even more obnoxious bastards like Justin Bieber.

Get some fucking headphones you disgrace for an Australian, I wanted to shout at him, but of course I am far too polite for that. The couple were on their way down from Everest Base Camp, so naturally they thought they were better than everyone else on their way up. The obnoxious lady did the rounds, moving from person to person and offering advice. She walked past me and I glared at her. She kept walking. *Good choice lady.*

An American woman – a real eccentric hippy type – leapt off the bench and made for the open floor, and then right there in the middle of the dining room began practising yoga. I felt sorry for the people eating lunch who had to swallow their food while her old, saggy butt was in their faces, executing the downward facing dog pose. Then she quickly changed her pose and almost knocked a big plate of Dal Bhat out of the waiter's hands. That was it. This was too much for me.

'Where did you bring me, Subash?' I asked.

'What you means?'

'I mean this is like a bloody circus for old people. I'm going to my room.'

Chapter Nine

THE PATH TO NAMCHE BAZAAR

The next morning dawned as bright and beautiful as ever. For some inexplicable reason I ordered the apple porridge again, which came out in a watery slop and had much the same effect as the previous time. I was excited this morning. We were off to Namche Bazaar. The general consensus is that this is where the mountains truly begin. It did involve about 1000m of climbing that I wasn't too thrilled about, but I was optimistic nonetheless. I was packed, had eaten and was ready to go by 8am. The path quickly joined the Dudh Khosi River and we were to follow it for much of the morning. After a few minutes we came to a long suspension bridge, but were halted by the crossing of one solitary mule. I'd already removed my jacket in anticipation of the long, warming climb ahead, but now standing in the shade I began to shiver. Frost lining the ground indicated it was still below freezing. I began jumping from foot to foot in an effort to warm myself. Subash looked at me like I was mad.

I distracted myself with the view. Immediately off to our right a pine-clad, v-shaped valley dropped down to meet the white water rapids that had shaped it across the vastness of time. Framed in a near-perfect mirror image was a snow-dusted pyramidal peak soaring high above into a cloudless sky. The valley and the mountain formed a diamond shape that was intersected by a horizontal ridgeline, almost forming a line of reflection. It was just a remarkable piece of geology.

For the next 30 minutes or so the path was most enjoyable. We went a little up followed by a little down. It was even fairly level for a time. The river below was positively roaring. We crossed back over the river, something that we were to repeat a fair number of times. We joined a section that was made up of perfectly rounded stones and we had to be careful where we placed our feet. This was ankle rolling country. We were surrounded on both sides of the river by rhododendron and pine forests, and we could have almost been in Europe.

A suspension bridge loomed high above us. That was to be our last crossing of the Dudh Khosi River, Subash told me, but first we had to climb up to it. On the bridge I got stuck behind a little old lady carrying way too much rice on her back. I would struggle with such a load over such a long distance. She was groaning under the strain and was moving pitifully slowly. I did feel sorry for her, but at the same time I did just kind of want to get off that bridge. Suspended high up on a rickety old suspension bridge, hundreds of feet above ice-cold glacial melt water doesn't strike me as the safest of places to be stuck.

The wind was howling down the valley, sending the thousands of prayer flags lining the bridge into a state of delirium. It was bitterly cold and my beanie was almost wrenched from my head on several occasions. The bridge was swaying slightly. I looked down. It was a long way down. Even if you somehow managed to survive the fall, you'd end up in the glacial melt water, catch pneumonia or hyperthermia and die. I glanced up to Subash who had overtaken the old lady, but there was no way I was getting around her. He was gesturing for me to look around and take in the view. I put on a fake smile and nodded my head, but dared not take my eyes from where I was placing my feet. On the other side, safe and sound, the little old lady put down the sack of rice with a terrible groan. I gave her a sad face, but she just hawked and spat on the ground, picked up the sack like it was a teddy bear and climbed stoically upwards.

This was the start of the climb and it was hard work. I was to some degree prepared, this being somewhere around the tenth day in a row I had been trekking. One by one we picked off all the people that had arrived by plane from Lukla and soon there were no tourists in front of us. The path was sufficiently wide enough to easily overtake the masses of porters carting goods up to Namche Bazaar. This path was a little uncertain what form it wanted to take. It kept changing from fixed stone stairs to loose scree, to just plain old dirt, while other areas were so overwhelmed with tree roots protruding from underground that they formed their own sort of stair system.

About half way up we came across two girls selling mandarins. Subash treated me, so I sat there sweating, catching my breath and enjoying beyond words the sweet flavour of fresh fruit. It was delicious.

'Only a gradual up from here,' Subash said.

'I don't believe you.'

'Yes really man it is a true,' he assured me.

'Yes but you have said that before and we still had 400 vertical metres to climb, and by rights we should have had abseiling equipment.'

'That was a gradual up also man.'

'That,' I paused for effect, 'was like climbing a ladder.'

'That was the Nepali flat man,' he said, looking deflated, and I felt good about it. He had raised my hopes for the last time. Sure enough, the gradient changed not one bit. It was as steep and tiresome as ever. We plodded on, rhythmically, as was our style, until eventually we plopped onto a large square flat area with a set of loos and another group of girls selling mandarins. *What's going on here?* I wondered why there were trekkers of different nationalities sprawled around the place.

One of the older girls immediately took a liking to me and so she began to hassle me. I am a sweater. There is no hiding from that fact. Always have sweated heaps, and always will. This day was no exception. I was absolutely drenched and my face looked like it had just been submerged in a lake.

Speaking in Nepali, the girl went on a huge rant at me. Funnily enough, I think I knew what she was saying. It went something like this:

'Excuse me sir. Are you aware that there is a great deal of water coming out of your face? In Nepal, we only have one cure for this foreigner disease. It is your lucky day. It comes in the form of this lovely mandarin and I happen to have a whole basket for sale right here.'

'No thanks, I already had one down there,' I said, pointing back down the trail.

'Just one sir? One is not enough to cure this illness.'

'No really, thanks. *Puyo* (meaning *I've had enough*). I don't want. There is no cure for this,' I added, circling my sweaty face with my pointing finger.

I looked up at Subash and he was laughing hysterically.

'What?'

'I think she likes you man. And it was like you know what she was saying. You guys having perfect conversation in different languages.'

'Whatever. What is this place?'

'This is a second Everest viewing place.'

'Why didn't you tell me?' I asked.

'Surprise.'

I grabbed my camera and followed Subash over to a ledge. There was a small window between two large pine trees, and there she was. Chomolungma, 'The Goddess Mother of the World', sat much closer this time, with her bodyguard Lhotse on her shoulder. She was conjuring some magic with the clouds above her. Lhotse, at 8516m (27939ft), was perched on the right-hand side and appeared and disappeared in wisps of swirling cloud, while Everest had cloaked herself in a dome of fluffy cloud. The dome sat there like a cape, seeming not to move; then very suddenly, Everest wished to be viewed no longer. It was as though she had suddenly sucked the dome forth, and within seconds she had disappeared completely. The jagged summit of Lhotse, the world's fourth highest mountain, poked her head through the clouds, as if to keep an eye on us. If we'd arrived 10 minutes later, Subash would have pointed into a white wall and announced that somewhere in that direction, we could have seen the goddess mother.

I turned to see that Nima had already remounted my backpack and was halfway up the next visible ascent, so I duly grabbed my day pack and began to follow him. It didn't take a great deal of time before a few stone buildings came into view, and before long we were staring at a town built on a steep slope, in the most unlikely of locations. Often described as a 'natural amphitheatre', Namche Bazaar is built on the side of a hill that curves around the township, and with the terraces for farming suspended above the settlement, it is easy to see why people call it so.

The buildings were either blue, red or green and the lodges were of a completely different scale from anything I'd seen thus far. As we made our way through the town, dozens of trekker shops lined the pavement. We passed a pub. We passed well-stocked shops with fruit and vegetables. It wasn't quite the Las Vegas I had in mind, but they had internet. Yes, internet. And telephones! I could find out rugby and cricket scores. I could reconnect with loved ones. I couldn't wait.

'Our lodge is just up here,' said Subash as I struggled my way up an incredibly steep final few stairs. Sitting on the veranda of our intended lodge were Dale and Andy, playing a game of cards with the Swedish blokes.

'Well if it isn't Seabass, Nemo and Mr Alex,' laughed Dale. 'What the hell happened to you?'

I explained my plight while Subash went to find me a room, but came back with a grave-looking face.

'I'm so sorry Gorong, but there is the no vacancy here.'

'I don't care mate, take me somewhere better. There are hundreds of lodges here. Give me Wi-Fi and a hot shower and I will be a happy man.'

I took my leave from my past travelling companions and we climbed even further into the town. Before long I'd checked into a place and was enjoying the sensation of removing my boots from my wrinkled, white feet.

Chapter Ten

ACCLIMATISING IN NAMCHE

Some major catastrophe always seems to befall the world when I go off the radar for a while. This time was no different. I entered into a world where flight MH370 had completely vanished, just days after I had flown Malaysian Airlines out of Kuala Lumpur. I was quite shocked that such an event could happen so near to me while I was utterly oblivious to it. I guess it really hit home just how remote my location was over the past fortnight.

Australia had wiped the floor with cricket's top ranked test side, South Africa, while my rugby team, the Queensland Reds, had recorded their first victory of the season. I checked my emails, let everyone know I was still alive and kicking, and other than having a heaven-sent, steamy-hot shower, I did nothing for the rest of the day.

I was to spend two nights in Namche Bazaar, the idea being altitude acclimatisation purposes. So, after sleeping quite well, Subash and I began an acclimatisation climb the following morning. It was hard work. It was steep, the trail was plagued by masses of loose rock, the air was cold and beginning to thin and I was just entirely buggered from the day before. We climbed out of Namche and after perhaps 15 minutes we overtook a group of three American men, perhaps in their mid-twenties.

It really is hard work overtaking someone at this altitude and on such a steep slope, because not only do you have to go past them, but you have to make sure you put enough distance between you and them before having a rest and a chance to catch your breath. Otherwise you have the ignominy of them catching and overtaking you once more. Then you have to wait for a time until the path is suitably wide and safe for you to overtake them once more; and heaven forbid, that may be a fair while away.

I climbed for perhaps three minutes without pausing to distance myself from the yanks. I turned around, realised they weren't in sight and then slumped down onto a boulder, barely able to suck oxygen into my lungs. We were perhaps at 3700m (12150ft) and I could really feel the air beginning to thin. I sat there for a good long while, wondering how long it would be before the Americans came into view and I'd have to get up and keep on going. But they never came. *Must have turned around.*

Eventually I got back on my feet and plodded on. As we took the final few steps and gained the ridge, I was treated to my first real Himalayan view. Immediately in front of me sat Ama Dablam, (6812m, 22350ft) my personal favourite mountain of all time. What a moment it was. Everest and Lhotse could be seen gracing the northern-most horizon, while Taboche Peak (6542m) stabbed the sky in the forefront of the picture. South of Ama Dablam we had the epic, fish-tail summit of Kangtega (6782m) and her Siamese twin sister, Thamserku (6608m), joined at the hip by a monstrous ridgeline. Looking back across the steepest valley yet – back over the top of the now invisible Namche Bazaar – we could see, through the lightest of hazes, Kongde (4250m) and Nupla (5885m). Take your pick. I had an awe-inspiring, 360-degree view of some of the most famous mountains on the planet, and it was just Subash and myself there to take it all in. I smiled, then laughed. This is what it's all about.

We sat on the mound for a good thirty minutes, snapping pictures and loving life. I gave Subash my camera with the largest lens and he enjoyed using it as a telescope, zooming in on the surrounding summits. I was a bit obsessed with Ama Dablam, with its two peaks and a mighty glacier flowing down between them. There are mountains, and then there are *mountains*, and Ama Dablam had an utterly unique shape. It stood by itself, unjoined to any other mountain, while its proud pyramidal prominence rose confidently over the valley. It was hard to pry myself away from that view, but eventually my stomach grumbled and I had to leave in search of sustenance.

On our way down we saw six Nepali men running (yes, running) up the slope towards us. We were descending via a different path to get a slightly different view, but we stopped now to watch them. As they came close enough for conversation, Subash stopped one of them and asked them what all the commotion was about. The man spoke for a good two minutes in Nepali (unbelievably, he wasn't even out of breath) before turning his back on us to sprint up the slope and catch his mates.

'What the hell is going on, Subash?'

'You remember those American trekkers we is going past?'

'Yeah I remember, I think they turned around.'

'No, one of them is falling,' he said. 'Maybe just after we is going past them. One of them is falling more than 10 metres and he is breaking his legs. So now they must carry him to the flat ground for helicopter back to the Kathmandu.'

'Oh shit, do they need any help?'

'Nothing we can be doing man,' he said, matter-of-factly.

We carried on, taking extra care to place our feet on sturdy rocks.

'You have to make the smart choices in the Himalaya,' Subash said after a while.

'I am a smart man,' I answered him. He gave me a dubious look, followed by a gentle smile. We walked past a Buddhist prayer wheel about the size of a house, and it took both of us to spin it. It was very satisfying when the wheel completed a full rotation, announced by the ringing of a bell, and we both began softly chanting *'Om Mani Pädme Hum',* sending out positive thoughts to the injured trekker.

*

Back in Namche, I spent the afternoon getting a longer and warmer sleeping bag, as well as a down jacket. My jacket was pretty good, but I was unsure how it would fare against -30°C weather. I bought some more hand sanitiser, had a fight with the ATM that only allowed me to take out $100 at a time, stocked up on Snickers Bars and then basically just chilled out.

I found a dish called 'rosti' on the menu, which was essentially deep-fried potato with flour and a couple of fried eggs on top. It was exquisite. Whoever cooked it should go on Masterchef Nepal. It was a meal that combined pure stodge with pure protein. It was nothing short of a trekking masterpiece.

'Hey Gorong, excuse me very much,' Subash interrupted me while I was doing some writing. 'Gorong, today is the last of the days where the drinking of the beer or the alcohol is allowed. Tomorrow we is going up high into the mountains, and alcohol is no good for the mountain sickness. If you is drinking the alcohol, you is getting the dehydrate, and is getting the mountain sickness for sure.'

'Well we better have a drink then!' I said while slamming my laptop case shut. I don't need much of an excuse to have a drink at the best of times, but heading into the mountains for two weeks of tee totalling is definitely a reason to drink.

'What is the local rum they have here, mate?'

'This is the Kukri Rum. It is meaning "dagger".'

'Sounds great, should we drink some of that?'

'Ok man.' He grinned and went over to order us some drinks. It was great having a guide. From getting a room for the night, to covering the bill, to ordering food and drinks, Subash did it all. He checked the bill thoroughly every morning to ensure they weren't trying to overcharge me, dealt with the locals for me when they couldn't speak English, and took control of every police or army checkpoint situation when they needed to see my permits. He did everything.

He returned with two glasses of streaming rum.

'You drink warm beer, now you're telling me you drink boiling hot rum too?' I asked him with one eyebrow raised higher than the other.

'Is the Nepali way!' he laughed. 'Is the Kukri Rum with hot water.'

'Ok,' I grimaced. 'Cheers!'

Well it wasn't too bad. It instantly warmed, nay, scorched my insides, but the taste was actually quite pleasant. I had one of them, and then informed Subash we would be having the second one with coke. The Australian way.

'I don't like man, it's too cold,' he said, and I laughed so hard I almost spat rum and coke across the room. I finished his and told him to go up and order another hot one for himself.

'Is that the local rum?' an Australian man asked me from another table a few metres away from us.

'Yeah, mate.'

'Is it any good?'

'Yeah it's actually pretty good with coke, I'm quite surprised.'

'When in Namche Bazaar,' he answered, and went off to order himself one. I got talking to him and his friend. They were Steve and

Rob, firefighters from Melbourne. They were also attempting the Three Passes Trek, but were planning to do it the opposite way, attempting the incredibly difficult and dangerous Kongma La pass first. They wanted to do it without either a guide or a porter.

Subash was listening intently to our conversation, but couldn't take it any longer.

'You is crazy to do Kongma La pass first.'

'But the guidebook says it is better to go that way because you don't gain the altitude too quickly,' said Rob. 'The way you are going, you go up too quickly.'

'Namche 3600, Thame 3800, Lumde 4300, Gokyo 4800,' stated Subash in the bluntest of ways possible. 'You tell me, guide of Nepal, how this is too much quickly.'

Subash was offended, and I could see why. How would two blokes from a 'flat country' know more than Subash about altitude sickness? When they didn't answer him, he continued. 'Kongma La pass may not even be opens now. So you want to go over there with no guides, no porters and you want to open up the pass with a new track? I think you very stupid.'

He turned and put his back to the chair once more and folded his arms. I put my hand on his shoulder and he immediately calmed down. I raised my glass and we did a 'cheers' and carried on drinking.

Four Virgin Australia air hostesses on their way down from Everest Base Camp checked into the lodge, came into the dining room and got talking to Steve and Rob. They told them a story of a rugby team that were on their way up the mountain. They said that the boys, in an attempt to prove how 'macho' they were, ignored all AMS safety procedures and tried to get to Base Camp as fast as their legs would take them. Apparently, every single one of them succumbed to mountain sickness and had to be airlifted back to the capital. In return, the firefighters told stories of fire- fighting. They were people, you see, that lived and breathed their jobs, and therefore had nothing else to talk about.

'Remember that car we found that time on the road that had that blue-healer dog trapped it in?'

'Oh yeah that time I had to get a grinder and cut the roof off?'

'Yeah that time. It was awesome hey?'

'Yeah.'

'What about that time a cat got stuck up that palm tree, but we didn't have a long enough ladder to get it?'

'Oh yeah, that time we had to go back to the station and get a bigger ladder?'

'Yeah that time, we never used a ladder that big before.'

'What do you do for work, Gordo?'

'Build roads.'

'Oh how interesting. Steve remember that time that bitumen tanker crashed and...'

I rolled my eyes at Subash, being ever so glad he was there for company. The hostesses left (I don't blame them) and Rob and Steve began talking amongst themselves. After a while Steve announced, 'Sorry Gordo, think we will be following you round like a bad stink. We've decided we will take your guide's advice and go around the other way.'

Perfect I thought, and then I was treated to an *epic* tale involving water *actually* being *deliberately* placed on fire.

*

We almost had a full guesthouse in Namche on that second night. A group of nine Koreans checked in, along with the four Virgin

Australia air hostesses, a solitary German man, the two Melbournian firefighters, two Italians blokes and all the accompanying guides and porters. What a noise emanated from that place that night. My goodness gracious me. You would have thought these people were adults, but someone needed the toilet every 15 minutes. Combine that with a few, rickety stories knocked together with creaky wood, and you have the perfect recipe for an appalling night's sleep

I had my new sleeping bag though and I was warm and cosy, so it didn't bother me too much I suppose. If I was awoken, I'd casually fondle around in the dark until I heard the rustling sound of a zip-lock bag, sneak my hand inside and help myself to a delicious sugarless vitamin C tablet. I'm not sure how good it is for one to gorge on those things, but I didn't have a cold.

Chapter Eleven

INTO THE MOUNTAINS

I had a late breakfast that morning of rosti and two fried eggs. Loaded up with energy, and wondering why on earth I'd just paid $100 to stay in a room the size of a double bed, I skipped eagerly into the waiting sun. I immediately pulled off my jacket and tied it to my backpack, then hit the trail with the keenness of a man that knows he is embarking on his easiest trekking day in a month. We steeply climbed the steps out of Namche Bazaar, our path well and truly deserted, as the 'Khumbu Highway' carried on north, bee-lining for Base Camp. As we approached the final turn that would see Namche fall out of sight, the roar of a helicopter's propellers came into earshot, and we stood gobsmacked as the machine took off from a pad about 100 metres ahead of us, before soaring what felt like inches from our heads. Subash and I looked at each other, shrugged our shoulders and carried on trekking. A few minutes later we heard the sound of horse hooves from up ahead. A moment later a soldier in full battle kit tore around the corner on bareback, and without even acknowledging our existence he took off at full speed. I had taken the lead (Subash needed to relieve himself) when I was startled half to death by a screaming sound. I looked up at where the sound had come from, and staring me dead in the eye was a green-looking pheasant. It was a good-looking bird. I reached for my camera, but the bird had already gone.

'It's all happening today,' I said to Subash as he joined me once more.

The path was pretty flat. I wasn't even becoming Nepalised, it just was. We could see our target for the night, Thame (pronounced Taamay), sitting a little higher than us on the other side of the valley, I'd say about 5 kilometres away. It did look very close indeed. The dusty track initially descended from the helipad through dry-looking pines trees that were interspersed by the occasional Juniper bush. The little shade we were blessed with did wonders on a day that was fast heating up. On the left, Nupla rose dramatically up before disappearing into some rare early morning cloud. Along the valley floor the river Bhote Kosi roared, causing masses of erosion just below the path. Huge sections of hill-face had simply broken off and collapsed into the valley. It was quite ugly if I'm being truthful.

We came across the village of Thamo, where we found a nice old lady that was prepared to make us a cup of tea (I say *us* because Subash, Nima and myself were now on the same schedule as the two firefighters). We sat in the sunshine and sipped at our tea while taking in the spectacular view of Thamserku and friends standing guard at the end of the valley.

After tea, we continued to drop down until we joined a fairly old-looking bridge, the only thing separating us from the violent white water rapids below. Painted on the cliff face were several different Buddhist figures of different colours.

'The green Buddha will be watching,' said Subash.

'Is that meant to be scary?'

'No!' he laughed. 'You watch, the green one is looking like it sees you everywhere you go.'

Sure enough, we walked along the face, but only the green one watched me pass. And then it was all the way up to Thame. It was probably only 40 minutes of climbing. It was pretty much straight up, but that didn't worry me anymore. My legs were strong and I was well acclimatised to this altitude. I got into my plodding rhythm and barely stopped on my way to the top. The firefighters were a long way behind by the time we were half way up. We came across several little open stone buildings that housed a multitude of prayer wheels, which we dutifully spun while chanting 'Om Mani Pädme Hum'.

Then we were in Thame, elevation 3800 metres, and what a lovely little place it was. Even though we had walked further away from Thamserku, it stood at the end of the valley, and a trick of the eye made it look bigger than ever. The town was built on a rare patch of fairly flat ground. Their greatest natural resource, stone, had been put to near obsessive use, as stone walls were everywhere, and divided almost anything that was divisible. As we strolled through town a pair of ladies were sat in the dirt in the middle of a small paddock, and were digging with their hands to unearth a crop of potatoes. Similar fields of dust were scattered around the area.

In a place as remote as this, you must be self-sustainable. As we continued, we came across the school and the Sunshine Lodge, a quaint looking building with a backdrop as spectacular as anything you will ever see. Patches of snow were dotted around the place, indicative that the temperature never really gets above freezing at this time of year.

I enjoyed a generous plate of Dal Bhat, washed down with four cups of ginger and lemon tea, before spending the afternoon just standing in the front courtyard in the sun and thinking to myself how lucky I was to be in such a beautiful place. I stood there all afternoon, just lapping it all up, as content as a man could be.

Later on, sat in the dining room, a solo Israeli trekker came barging in and introduced himself to everyone. He all but slapped my book out of my hand so that he could shake it. The serenity of my afternoon had just taken a turn for the worst.

'Ok my friend, I have a big plan for us,' he said.

'For us?'

'Yes. Tomorrow you and me, we get some crampons and an ice axe. I already spoke with the owner, he tells me he can rent me some for the day. Then we will go and climb that mountain behind Thame for an acclimatisation day. What you think?'

'I think you're crazy mate,' I answered him in a matter-of-fact-cum-utterly-bemused kind of way.

'No, it will be perfect. We can trek and still get to conquer a mountain in the Himalaya.'

'Do you ever really *conquer* the mountain?' I asked in an attempt to change the subject.

'Yes man. And it is 5300 metres, so we will already have the perfect acclimatisation for the Renjo La pass. Can't you see it's perfect?'

'No it's not perfect. I am a trekker, not a mountaineer. I came here to see the mountains, not to climb them.'

'But it's ok,' he retorted. 'We will have an ice axe and crampons.'

'I've never used an ice axe or crampons before, have you?'

'No man, but we'll figure it out. And the owner of the lodge said I won't even need the ice axe and crampons.'

'Then why did you still hire them?'

'You know, in case of an emergency.'

'Honestly mate, I think you're a bloody idiot and I'm not going anywhere with you,' I said abruptly, getting a bit frustrated. At the time, I wrote in my travel journal: *Israeli idiot came barging in, such a wanker that I can't even bother to write about him now.*

He actually wanted me to change my entire schedule, including flights from Lukla, just so that I would climb a mountain with him that he knew absolutely nothing about. We went outside and he pointed to the mountain.

'Sir, sir,' said Nima. 'Taking ice axe crampons but gimble gongle mountain black rock.'

Nima burst out laughing and I joined in. The Israeli had no crampon or ice-axe experience, but was going to rent both from the lodge anyway, even though the lodge owner, a former porter and mountain climber had told him it was unnecessary. Now we could see the peak and there wasn't a single ice cube on it.

'It's people like him that get mountain sickness,' Steve said, and I had to agree.

*

I woke up with glorious sunshine radiating through the window and warming the room completely. I shoved off the sleeping bag and just lay there absorbing its warmth. I must have laid there for a good 20 minutes before I summoned the strength to move. I felt hung-over. It wasn't fair. I had been drinking nothing but tea choc-full of goodness, had a nutritious meal in dhal bhat and I'd had a record amount of sleep, but still felt worse for wear. Clearly it was the altitude.

Subash had forced me to eat a bowl of garlic soup for breakfast, which was delicious and good for high altitude adaptation, but it repeated on me all morning and was a monumental error in judgement. I vowed to keep eating garlic soup, but perhaps just before bed time. We left Thame at about 9am, a late start by our standards, and were soon gasping for breath on the ascent out of the town. We paused regularly, but we probably would have done that anyway due to the spectacular view presenting itself all around us. We gained the top after 5 or 10 minutes, before entering some gradually undulating terrain.

We spent the day following the river up along the bottom of the valley, which was quite small by Himalayan standards. Hills rose on either side of us, but the maximum width of the valley couldn't have been more than 2 kilometres. We were entering a real barren looking place. The hills were brown and seemingly lifeless, and erosion was prevalent with vast quantities of hillside simply disappearing onto the valley floor. The presence of the occasional juniper tree was hardly enough to bind this soil together. The view was brown and white. It looked like a desert.

After climbing gradually up for about half an hour, we came across a large herd of yaks being taken up into the mountains. There were probably 30 of them in total. We approached them on a narrow ledge and had to match their grinding pace until the path widened out onto the valley floor. It was good to watch. Everyone – guides, porters and trekkers – suddenly became yak herders. We'd passed an Englishman named Michael and his daughter Juliet just moments earlier, and I noticed Juliet getting involved, shouting 'Yaahh' and waving her arms at a slow yak. It was fun.

At some point during the stroll we ascended past the 4000m mark, and we congratulated ourselves. At midday the tiny town of Marulung came into sight and it presented a welcome tea break. A sign informed us that we had ascended to an altitude of 4200m. I'd earned myself a snickers bar. I sat there for perhaps 20 minutes talking with Michael and Juliet, before they decided to press on to the destination, Lungden, for lunch. I had a lot of clothes on, but I was beginning to feel dangerously cold.

'Subash I'm leaving!' I called inside the only lodge in town, grabbed my bag and actually began jogging along the path. In about two and a half seconds I was out of breath, and so I continued on at a normal pace. The next town presented a height gain of only 150m, but what a difference it made. I soon rounded up Michael and Juliet even though they had left about 10 minutes earlier than me. They were struggling whereas before they were skipping up the valley.

My head became light, and I had that surreal feeling back; the one I had experienced when I was sick all those days ago. It didn't worry me too much. I did a quick are-you-drunk test like you see in American movies, and after coming to the conclusion that I still had my coordination, I carried on. My legs again felt like they didn't belong to me, but they were light and pain free. I got my breathing into a good, steady rhythm and then just plodded on for Lungden.

By the time we were there, my head was light and I felt like I'd just come from an opium den. It was the first time I had really noticed the effects of the altitude. I had a slight headache. We were now at 4350m, and had ascended 1000m in two days. We were already above the recommended acclimatisation line. Subash wanted to hit the Renjo La Pass the next day at 5300m, before descending down to Gokyo to sleep, which sits at 4800m, a height gain of 1400m in three days.

I knew we were now hard-pressed for time, but I didn't want to risk my health in the high Himalaya. We had already stretched our limits and I could feel it. Going up again the next day would have been a terrible idea, and gone against every single bit of literature I had read on AMS up until that point. We were due to have a rest day in Gokyo as there is a great deal to see and do there, but I was concerned I would already be way too high above my acclimatisation line. Everyone else attempting the pass, Michael, Juliet, Steve and Rob were staying in Lungden for an acclimatisation day.

We sat in the lodge in Lungden and I tried my best to seem normal, even though my head was swimming. There were only two lodges in a town consisting of only four-or-so buildings, and only one of which was open. A lifeless yak-dung stove sat in the middle of the room, on top of which sat a pot of water that had frozen over completely.

Subash brought out my small pot of lemon and ginger tea and then unfolded a large map of the region out on the table.

'Today we are here,' he said, pointing to Lungden on the map. 'Tomorrow we go over the Renjo La Pass here, before going downs to Gokyo. We are spendings the two nights there.'

'What about...' I said slowly, knowing that he wasn't going to like this. 'If we don't spend two nights in Gokyo, but instead spend two nights here to acclimatise.'

'Here man? There is a nothings here.'

'Yeah I know but I can already feel the effects of altitude, what happens if I go up another 400 metres and it gets worse?'

The best thing about the argument that ensued was that he knew I was right. I had an argument based on science, while he had a schedule to keep. I'm happy to report that common sense prevailed and we scheduled the extra day.

*

I woke at 6am and it took a concentrated effort to crawl out of my sleeping bag. I fumbled around in my backpack for my little thermometer, switched it on and was horrified to read -12°C. I shivered (more to do with the thought of it being that cold than anything else), chucked on every bit of clothing I could find, and then made for the toilet. I had a leak (took me a good few minutes to find it), then realised the water for flushing, sitting in a bucket to the side of the toilet, was completely frozen. So I gingerly left the bathroom hoping that no one would see me exit. I crawled back into bed to continue to read my book, *The Snow Leopard* by Peter Matthiessen, although I can honestly say I thought it was an atrocious piece of literature.

I was the first up in the morning and soon found the lady of the house pottering around in the kitchen. I ordered a small pot (about 5-6 cups) of ginger and lemon tea, along with a vegetable omelette with chapatti bread. I felt pretty damn good. It didn't take long for the place to fill up. First Juliet came through followed by Michael, then a German couple surfaced that very much kept to themselves. The firefighters were the last to emerge, and my breakfast was done and dusted by the time they had ordered.

'What about that time in station 29 when all that chocolate rocked up?' said Rob.

'Oh yeah, that time!' said an enthused Steve.

'What happened?' Juliet asked, and I could have taken my shoe off and thrown it at her.

'Oh you see, as we're emergency services, we get chocolate at discount prices,' Rob began, but I'd had enough of these clowns and it was barely 7am. I knew everyone was essentially planning to walk together this morning for our acclimatisation climb so I pestered Subash, asking if he'd finished his breakfast yet.

'Today the Nima will be the guide,' he informed me. 'Today I is resting so the Nima will show you the ways.'

Well it was immediately taxing – the steepest climb that I had yet encountered. There was no path, so we made our own, and it was straight up. It would have been a lung-buster at sea level, let alone here at 4350m (14271ft) above it. Up and up we went until after barely a few minutes the little community of Lungden had taken the form of a few little red and blue dots. I'm not going to lie, I was pretty pissed off.

'Nima this is meant to be a rest day,' I said

'Yes sir, rest day.'

'Yes but this isn't resting man, this is bloody exhausting. I am meant to be going over a 5300 metre pass tomorrow, and you choose this opportune moment to unleash the steepest, most dangerous part of the trail in two weeks?'

'Ah sir, resting no good sir. On day this chunga bunga walking some is better sir.'

The ligaments in my ankles were sore. It was so steep that even standing in a stationary position, catching my breath, still managed to put all the strain on my muscles and ligaments. Every ounce of my strength was spent hanging precariously to the side of that steep hill.

'Sir little bit a more and top and very good a view sir.'

'Ok I believe you,' I said, while thinking: *Wait til I see you Subash. I am going to kill you. We get to Namche Bazaar and Nima has a rest day while we go gallivanting up some massive steep mountain. The view was pretty good though. Now I want nothing more than a rest day and instead you give me the hardest day of the trek so far, while you sit on your arse and send Nima off to guide me instead. I'm going to give you a piece of my mind Subash Gurung. Holy shit, stop whinging. What's wrong with you?*

Then I just kind of stopped whinging. I felt better. I carried on climbing. I slowed down the pace and entered Gordon's special plodding mode. Immediately I was out of breath, but at least I began to find a little of that rhythm that was impossible to find when I was angry. We joined this kind of gully area that was laced with large, unstable looking boulders, but we continued to climb them nonetheless and they held strong. After a good 10 minutes the slope began to ease off, although the same could not be said for my breathing, which carried on like the clappers. *Only a few more steps to go* I thought, and before I knew it there was nowhere else to climb.

I stood immobilised by the sight in front of me. Rising in front of me was one, two, three, four, five jagged peaks, too steep for the accumulation of snow, while a couple of the less-vertical rises were laced with deep snow and ice. Slowly I turned around. Mountain upon mountain rose sharply from the depths of the valley floor. Mount Numbur peaked its beautiful head over the top of an unusually low ridgeline. We had another 360-degree panorama of the most formidable, astonishing beauty; and once again, save for my little Sherpa friend, the view belonged to me alone. The sound of silence was almost deafening.

147

Nima had taken a slightly different path and was snapping a few photos on his phone. I burst out into the laughter of a crazy person. We were now at about 4600m above sea level, and if Mont Blanc was somehow moved here and placed next to us, the summit would almost be in reach. I had 20 snow-capped peaks greater than 6000m right in front of me, almost close enough to touch, and it was all mine. I sat on the only rock big enough to protrude the surface of the snow, and just lapped it all up. Nima joined me, and we began a frenzy of photo snaps. I just could not get over the fact that it was only us there. The brilliant blue of the sky was not disrespected by one single cloud. Not one. We climbed over the top of the flat hill and made our way carefully across 100 metres of soft, deep, melting snow. I followed Nima's footsteps exactly, but where he remained on the surface, I always broke through, sometimes to knee depth. *You little bloody elf!* I thought to myself.

We were going downhill now, but my heavy breathing rate returned within seconds. Having gotten off the snow, we rounded a little bend, and Lungden reappeared back into sight, but it was impossibly far away. How had we come that distance? My head began spinning with the accumulative expenditure of energy, just as it had done the day before. It was time to get back and really rest. It didn't take long to descend. We walked through a farmer's field and came across the biggest pile of yak shit I had ever seen. Scrap that, it was the biggest pile of any kind of shit I have ever seen. I saw Subash and didn't give him a piece of my mind. I was elated.

I grabbed a Snickers Bar and almost swallowed it whole, grabbed my laptop and a bottle of water, and went outside to enjoy the last of the sunshine. The clouds were beginning to form around the highest peaks and I knew it wouldn't be long until it was absolutely bloody freezing again. I found a perfect leaning rock on a gentle slope, with patches of snow on either side of me, and plonked myself down in front of the best view I had ever seen in my life. I had it all to myself. I then began to write on a screen that I couldn't see from all the glarw, and wondered exactly how manu spelling mistakes I would have to correcr. I put my earphones in and began to play Clinton Fearon's epic song *Feelin' The Same*:

'On top of the mountain enjoying the morning sun

On top of a mountain having so much fun

On top of a mountain til the evening comes

On top of a mountain where pleasure's never done.

I'm feeling the freedom all around me,

And I hope, I hope, I hope that you're feeling the same!'

Chapter Twelve

ATTEMPTING THE RENJO LA PASS

We were awake at 4am on the 16th of March. It was a day that I was looking forward to, but at the same time I was nervous beyond belief. We were going to attempt the 5360m Renjo La Pass.

I forced down a huge breakfast of turmeric-fried potatoes with an omelette on top, knowing I would need every ounce of energy I could obtain. I washed it down with about a litre of lemon and ginger tea, finished packing my things, and we were ready to trek a little before 5am. It was pitch black, so we mounted our head torches and walked out the door.

It was bitterly cold. We walked out of Lungden over flat ground for perhaps only five minutes before the ascent began, and would not finish until we reached the pass in about a vertical kilometre's time. It was steep, walking over terrain similar to that of the acclimatisation trek the previous day. It did not take long for our eyes to adjust to the darkness, and after perhaps just 20 minutes into the walk we had all turned our head torches off.

The sun kissed the tops of the highest peaks behind us, which brought about a spectacular sunrise, but did little to ease the cold that had already seeped into our bones. The two firefighters had set a ferocious pace. At first I had tried to keep up with them, but I realised that it was going to be a long day and so I eased off and let them have it. My mouth had dried out due to the speed of my breathing and my tongue was beginning to stick to the roof of my mouth. I dropped my pack and reached for my bottle of water, opened the lid and tilted it, but nothing came out. I burst out laughing. The bottle had frozen solid. I'm glad I had seen the funny side of it otherwise I would have been pretty pissed off. I shoved the bottle inside my jacket, remounted my pack, and continued the steep climb.

The morning was absolutely stunning. A clearer, bluer sky I don't believe I have ever seen. The contrast created by the snow-capped peaks and the blue of the sky was magnificent. Subash pointed out a piece of poo on the ground and said that it belonged to the snow leopard. I was dubious - he was a trekking guide and not a biologist after all - but I nonetheless alerted myself to the possibility of spotting one of the rarest creatures on our planet.

By 7am we climbed over the top of a rounded ridge before entering a new world. It was still the ice age up there. The ground flattened off and the snow deepened to just below my knee. Over to my right a frozen lake glinted with a brilliant colour of turquoise while still more jagged peaks rose impossibly high above me. My poor neck copped a flogging in those days, always craning upwards to view the distant summits.

I had caught the two firies now. As I climbed over a stone wall, wondering who on earth had built it all the way up here, I caught sight of them and heard them in deep conversation. I wondered how on earth they could be talking in this rarefied atmosphere, where oxygen availability was rapidly approaching 50%. Far down below I could see Juliet and Michael just entering the flat section, where they flopped onto the ground for a much deserved rest. I walked with Steve and Rob now, who were blabbering on about all things work, so once again I just dropped off the pace a bit and let them have it.

It was still bitterly cold, despite the exertion required. I had icicles in my beard. Literally.

We climbed through a bit of snow around a blind blend and then saw a man below in the snowfields unpacking his tent. He had camped the night just short of 5000 metres above sea level. Brave man. We passed him and carried on up a gradually rising path. We climbed up probably 50m of steep slope over a mixture of rock, ice and snow, before being greeted by a frozen lake.

Subash informed me of the new milestone. We were 5000 metres above sea level. That is 16404 feet. It was time for a photo and a well-earned rest. There were plenty of boulders strewn around the place, so I perched myself there, ate two Snickers Bars and drank up the newly melted water. We were sitting in a magnificent basin with sharp arêtes making up about 300 degrees of the view, the other 60 being from where we had come; back down to the valley below. We could see Renjo La now. It looked awfully steep and far away. We were joined by Michael and Juliet, who were ecstatic they had caught up with the boys. It was short-lived though. They arrived and I got up and left.

At this altitude the going was incredibly tough. My breathing went back to normal at rest, but halfway through my first step I was gasping for air. I felt heavy. I weigh about 110kg and was carrying another 10 on my back, but it felt as though I was dragging a one-tonne slab of concrete with me up to the pass. I'd take five steps and pause for 30 seconds before taking five more. The going was agonisingly slow. It had been 10 minutes since I'd left the frozen lake. I collapsed on a rock for another 10 to rest. I was beginning to develop a serious headache that lined the top of my skull.

Subash hit a rock with his makeshift bamboo walking stick, which brought me back out of an oxygen-deprived trance. I got to my feet slowly and then began an even slower plod up the steep slope. My progress was glacial. I just could not believe that I could see the pass right there, and yet, as time moved mechanically onwards, I was not getting any closer. Every minute was agony. Every step was like playing an entire game of rugby. After another hour I was only halfway up from the lake. I collapsed on a rock and just sat there, dumbfounded by the difficulty of the task. My head felt as though it was about to explode and I had zero strength remaining.

I looked down the face of the cliff and I saw that Steve, Rob and the two poms were now walking together. Their progress was even slower than mine. I simply could not fathom that they were so far behind. They looked like little ants from way up here. They had left just after me, but were still at least 50 minutes behind. I carried on, utterly exhausted. We got to a point where I just collapsed in the snow and sat there stupefied, staring at Subash.

'Come on man, give me your bag,' he said.

'No way, you're not carrying mine as well.'

'No problem for me.'

'No way, I can do it,' I said defiantly.

'When I first start my working as porter, I carry 55kg of chickens on my back.'

I tried to imagine what that might look like, but couldn't. He broke into a smile and skipped down the 15-or-so metre distance that separated us, and before my brain could even find time to protest again, he had wrenched my bag from my weak grip, shouldered it, and began to climb again. Feeling a little bit useless, I got up, considerably lighter, and carried on once more. We zigzagged our way up, climbing through areas of deep, melting snow, over stone staircases and loose scree. I looked up and saw Nima hop over the last of the stairs. He had made the pass, but I had a long way to go.

An hour and a half after leaving the frozen lake, I hit the main wall of the pass, and just had one, agonising ascent to go. I sat down, again, for what might've been the 400th time. I looked down and saw the group below sitting in the same spot as they were about 20 minutes beforehand. I saw Steve and Rob stand up, shoulder their packs, and then carry on the wrong way. They were going back, just 100 metres shy of the pass. That's how hard the going was. Subash called down the mountain, issuing encouragement, but the firefighters just hung their heads and headed all the way back to Lungden. Juliet and Michael stood up, and we anxiously watched to see which way they would turn.

'Which way?' I asked Subash.

'They go up,' he said.

They seemed to stand there for ages, as if summoning strength, and then they continued to climb. We cheered for them, loudly, and we hoped that it spurred them onwards. It was now time for us to continue our own battle. I rubbed my head furiously, willing the pain away.

'If gets worse we go back,' Subash said.

'No way. I can see the pass. We continue.'

I'd needed a wee for a while now, but hadn't the energy to do so. However it was becoming unbearable, so I let Subash know my intention and cornered myself into the cliff-wall. I looked down and was utterly horrified to find that I was turning the snow an orangey-brown colour. I was dangerously, dangerously dehydrated. I grabbed my water bottle and sipped at it. Shaking it revealed I only had half-a-litre to last me the rest of the day. This wasn't good.

Step by step we continued, resting more than we moved. Nima came striding down the slope. Subash uttered something quickly to my porter, who happily nodded. The time was getting away from us. This time of year in the Himalaya, the mornings are almost always crystal-clear, but around late morning to early lunchtime the clouds begin to roll in and cloak the highest peaks.

'The pass is still clear,' said Subash. 'Only a little cloud around Lhotse.'

Without a word, Nima grabbed my day-pack from Subash, looked at me solemnly and nodded in encouragement before he turned and seemed to jog back up to the pass.

'Just three more minutes,' Subash encouraged.

Suddenly the wall on our right ended and I had nothing to lean on. At the top of about eight more stairs stood an untidy cairn wrapped in prayer flags that flapped furiously in the breeze. It was the Renjo La. I had made it.

I took the final stairs as though a weight had been lifted from me. Suddenly I became one of those sure-footed porters. I put my head down, so as not to see the view until I could see it in its entirety. I raised my head slowly, eyes open, and took in perhaps the greatest view in the world. A wall of mountains, boasting four 8000m peaks, loomed suddenly in front of me. Mountain after mountain, peak after peak, there stood the greatest wall, the greatest barrier I had ever seen, or will ever see again. Cho Oyo, Mount Everest, Lhotse and Makalu dominated the picture – four mountains in the top ten -

were spread across the entire horizon, and in between these peaks that were among the greatest on earth were hundreds of other peaks; impressive, but dwarfed.

Take anyone of those smaller peaks and move them to any other mountain range on earth, and they would be famous; but here they were children, servants that bowed down at the feet of their masters. Looking down into the valley was a great, frozen lake, one of the great spiritual lakes of Nepalese Buddhism, and further still, the icy settlement of Gokyo, where we would be heading that afternoon.

Glaciers crunched their way down icy slopes, churning up vast deposits of lateral moraine that provided trekkers with formidable barriers to overcome.

Subash and Nima rushed across and embraced me in the biggest, warmest hug I'd ever experienced. We locked arms in a small three-man circle and began dancing around and around in happiness.

'Sit, sit!' I heard Subash saying, and I obliged, parking myself on a rock ledge that had been built for this purpose. I was absolutely gobsmacked. I could not take my eyes off the view I front of me. It is the single greatest view a person can get of Mount Everest. Even from

Kala Pathar, where most people climb to see the greatest mountain on earth, you can only see a bit of the face and summit, whereas here, we saw the mountain rise from Gokyo at 4800m to its summit more than 4km higher.

As I sat on the wall, a camera was shoved into my hands. My camera. In the other hand a dry, stale piece of Tibetan bread. I tried to chew, but my mouth was far too dry. I put the bread down, and began taking photos, desperately trying to capture a picture that would do justice to what was standing before me. It felt as though I had been invited to the table to dine with the gods, and I did not want to upset them.

I reached for my water bottle and dribbled the last few drops into my already-barren mouth.

'How long down to Gokyo?' I asked Subash.

'Two hours maximum.'

'We better go mate, I'm already dehydrated and now I'm out of water.'

'Yes *jam jam (let's go)*,' he agreed.

I stood, regained control of my pack, and on exhausted legs we began the descent down a perilously steep path. It wasn't really a path, it was more like a few footprints in very deep snow. We were going down, but I was mimicking a free-diver that had just returned to the surface following a lengthy spell underwater. It was slippery and dangerous and I fell on numerous occasions. For an hour we made our way through the deep snow. If I strayed from the path even a millimetre, my leg would plunge down and I'd find myself waist deep in snow. The energy required to pull myself out was diminishing every time it happened.

We rested frequently despite the descent. As we came out of the deep snow, we entered a minefield of dangerously positioned rocks on steep slopes, none of which were sturdy. Subash looked down and muttered something in disgust. He later told me this wasn't the actual path. The path traced the bottom of the valley, but was in fact covered in about 10 feet of snow. So we scrambled over loose scree and dirt, falling frequently and taking the skin off my arms and legs.

I cursed often. Subash had never seen this side of me before. If I was fully rested and functioning properly, this still would have been a tall ask, but on oxygen-deprived and fatigued legs, this was dangerous. On several occasions I'd step on a rock that was just waiting for an invitation to be plunged into the valley below, and I'd oblige. The rock would begin its freefall, while I would be scrambling with my hands desperately trying to avoid the same fate.

Subash was very patient, realising the extent of my exhaustion. He was hungry and thirsty, too, and while my boots were Gore-Tex and waterproof, the fabric of his had absorbed the freezing-cold snow melt, and I could tell he was uncomfortable. I'd fall and just sit there for ages, staring as the clouds began to rapidly envelope the surrounding mountains. It was beginning to get cold.

'Come man, I take your bag again,' Subash said.

We had much the same argument that resulted in much the same outcome. I was just so thirsty, while my headache continued to get worse and worse. I took my water bottle and filled it with snow, hoping that it would melt to give me some reprieve. I fell again and again, and each time it was getting harder and harder to get up. My pants were beginning to rip. I rested often, usually after I had fallen on the ground, and didn't have the strength to get back up.

I came across Subash, who was sitting on a rock with a worried expression on his face. I carried on past him, entering a really steep section that was made up of just loose dirt that I slid down out of control. I lost about 50 metres of altitude in a few seconds and screamed out a word I'd rather not repeat, before getting up and falling over again. It was hell.

The snow began to melt in my bottle, but teasingly so, giving me only a drop at a time. My fortunes, however, began to change. We had lost a lot of altitude, and the path became a lot easier. It was now pretty much flat ground to walk over, with the occasional section of deep snow sitting in a sheltered area. The snow began to melt more in my bottle, and I really noticed the difference in my body with every sip of water. I even noticed the air begin to thicken and breathing became a lot easier. You know the oxygen is scarce when you descend to 4800 metres and the world suddenly seems to be positively teeming with air molecules.

We wandered over a well-worn trail and it was obvious that we had joined the route to Gokyo Ri, a popular viewpoint of Everest. We rounded a final hill and there was Gokyo, shimmering like a mirage at the end of a frozen lake. We came to a set of rock steps that were submerged to form a type of bridge over a section of water between two lakes, and I stepped over these with a great deal of care. Subash had gone ahead to organise a room, and we found him at the lodge.

'You made it man!' he cried out loud. I put my hand out to shake his and he slapped it away and gave me a hug.

'You are the very best Nepali Himalaya guide,' I said to him.

'Me? No! Maybe,' he answered and we both laughed.

'Thank you, Subash,' I said.

'No problem man, it's my job.'

'Well you're a guide and carrying my bag is not your job. So thank you. I won't forget it. I would not have been able to do that without you guys.'

'Listen,' he said, a little more seriously. 'I tell you something now. Like a little analyse of the day. You make it over the pass and other two Australian guys didn't. I tell you why. One, you made a good choices man. You walk in from the Jiri, so you fit and acclimatise much nicer than them. They is getting sick and going all the ways back, but they fly into Lukla at 2800 metres. This is no good. Second things is, you notice they is talking way too much. No oxygen is there, but they is talking anyway. This is a very tiring things man.

'I ask you *Teksa*? And you is saying to me: *Teksa*. Nothing else. Too much a talking at these altitudes tiring them out too much. Another things man, yesterday you is telling me now they is wanting the porters. But only for the pass. No porters just wanting job for one days going over the passes. You hire me and Nima, and this is a very good things for you. These are the differences man, and that is why tonight you is in Gokyo, and they go back to Lungden.'

There was no denying he was right. If I could go back and do the trip all again I would not have done it any other way (except maybe avoid the dhal bat from Nunthala). I had a very good guide and porter, both of whom were fast becoming my friends.

They ushered me into a very basic room made of glass and wood. I walked inside and it was instantly 10 degrees warmer than outside. It was a Gokyo sunroom. I ordered two bottles of water and a noodle and garlic soup. The owner of the lodge came down to meet me personally after hearing I was exhausted from crossing the pass, and he took my order and welcomed me to Gokyo and his lodge. It was all very nice. I smashed a litre of water in minutes and annihilated the garlic and noodle soup, which was delicious. I went up to my room to put on more clothes.

I was hydrated, my headache was slowly dissipating, I was warm, my room was large and comfortable and afforded brilliant views over the frozen lake, and I was about to get dinner and Wi-Fi. Was this heaven? I dined on a delicious vegetable curry, rich with chick peas, lentils, beans and spicy potatoes, let everyone in the outside world know that I was still kicking, then went to bed a contented man at about 7pm. I don't believe I moved a muscle for 11 hours.

Chapter Thirteen

GOKYO AND TRAVERSING THE NGOZUMBA GLACIER

I woke up at 6am, glanced at my thermometer and was horrified to read -9°C. The only thing exposed to the air was my nose, and I grabbed it worryingly, making sure it wasn't frozen solid. I breathed a deep sigh of relief. It was warm and runny. I made a quick movement to grab my iPod and then disappeared under the covers again. I listened to an entire reggae album, Clinton Fearon's *Me and Mi Guitar,* before I even considered moving again.

When the album had finished, I slowly moved the sleeping bag downwards and I could see glorious morning sunshine seeping in through the slits in the curtains. Another glance at the thermometer revealed it was -2.5 degrees. *That will have to do I'm afraid.* I threw off the sleeping bag, the exertion of which left me out of breath. I quickly layered up and then went to the dining room for some breakfast and ginger and lemon tea.

Somehow I was fully recovered from the day before. I wasn't sore or tired, I felt fit and ready to go. But I knew that after only two days I would be going through the same ordeal again, so I did absolutely nothing this day, and it was epic. I caught up on some writing. I watched with pity as people struggled up the huge lookout hill, Gokyo Ri. I'd asked Subash if it was worth climbing up and having a look, but he assured me the view from the Renjo La was very similar, but far more spectacular. I watched with interest as two French girls walked for 20 seconds before resting for 20 minutes. I knew how it felt, but they'd only just joined the bottom of the hill and had a long, long way to go. I sat in the dining room, put my photos onto my laptop, and then looked at them over and over again in awe. Did I really experience that view yesterday?

I ordered an early lunch of garlic soup and some kind of spaghetti with sauce that was pretty good, but not exceptional. I barely moved all day. I fetched my book, *The Snow Leopard*, an account of an expedition across Nepal and into Tibet to view the blue sheep in its natural habitat. It was a wild adventure, crammed with philosophy and religious teachings. Like the spaghetti, it was worth a go, without being a masterpiece. I know I earlier called it 'an atrocious piece of literature', but I was coming to the end now and looking forward to moving on to my next book (written in coherent English).

As night began to fall the temperature plummeted, but the giant steel heater in the middle of the room kept the place toasty. The Namaste Lodge was busy, and the room was almost completely full of people, adding to the warmth. It was so busy that unfortunately the porters were all kicked out to the adjacent room where there was no heating, but as people slowly trickled off to bed, the porters made their way back into the warmth, which added to the evening atmosphere.

Subash and a couple of the guides rounded up a pack of cards and brought them over to my table, and they began to do some magic tricks. Subash nailed one impressive trick the first time, but should have quit while he was ahead, because the second time he made an absolute meal of it. Hearing the commotion from the first time he did it, he now had a huge audience for the second time, comprising all the staff of the lodge and a large group of Korean trekkers. Needless to say he crumbled under the pressure and had everyone in stitches.

It was approaching 8pm. The sun had been gone for two hours now, and it was almost time for bed. I glanced at the outside thermometer on my way to bed, *only -5 degrees*. I climbed the stairs and dived into my sleeping bag. The first 10 seconds were torture, but by the time it had warmed up I was already asleep.

*

I awoke again, this time slightly confused. I looked up at the ceiling and saw a thousand panda bears surrounded by the Olympic rings. The words 'Beijing 2008' were sprawled everywhere. Ah yes, the décor for my little room in Gokyo. I was still in the Himalaya's, 4800m above sea level. The sun was already up; it was time I did the same. We were having a lazy morning and then going glacier walking. Should be interesting.

I dined on vegetable noodle soup for lunch, which was in fact instant two-minute noodles with some dried vegetables thrown in. I was then ready to check out of the Namaste Lodge, so I asked for my bill, and almost had a fit when told I had to pay US $120. The Wi-Fi service cost $10 a day and was so slow that most of the time I couldn't even use it. I charged my laptop twice and that cost me $15. What really concerned me, however, was that I had a good seven days left of trekking and there was no ATM or currency exchange place before I got back to Namche Bazaar. I'd have to be a bit more responsible.

We began the climb out of Gokyo at 12 noon. The sun was shining and the weather was warm, and I had dressed for the occasion. We negotiated some steep, slippery snowy rises before heading down onto the Ngozumba Glacier, a river of ice running from north to south, beginning further north up near Cho Oyu Base Camp. Far down the valley clouds were rapidly forming, and began to race each other towards where we were standing. I unpacked my camera and snapped a few pictures of the glacier, which was actually pretty damn ugly. The ice was dirty, and vast, vast quantities of moraine were scattered around, giving the area an almost lunar appearance. By the time I'd returned my camera to the safety of my bag, the clouds were upon us. They were moving that fast, and it had begun to snow ever so lightly. After ten minutes of scrambling over rocks, boulders and icy bits, the snow was really beginning to come down. I'm talking blizzard-esque.

The route was marked by small stones being piled on top of each other, and were clearly visible every 50 metres or so. However, we were now hiking in a cloud that was hell bent on burying us with snow and visibility was way less than 50 metres. I paused for a moment and considered my surroundings. It was so easy to follow a guide and I pretended for a second that Subash wasn't there, wondering which direction I would take. I scanned around, but there was no sign of stone piles. The heavy snow had even wiped out any trace of Subash's footprints, and he was standing only 10 metres in front of me.

'Jesus, I'd hate to be doing this trek today without a guide,' I called above the howl of the wind.

'Why you think peoples are going missing every year?' he called back.

We followed a bizarre route along the glacier and I stopped in my tracks every now and again to listen to the glacier creak and groan under my feet, a real reminder that we were treading on a moving river. Rocks perched high up on the steep slopes above us occasionally fell around us, sometimes a little too close for comfort. After about an hour and a half, we began a steep and tiring climb over loose scree, which saw us emerge onto some level ground.

'We are no longer on the glacier,' Subash said, and I did a little happy dance. I didn't really like it that much. The idea that we could fall into a hidden crevasse at any time, especially with visibility being so low, worried me slightly.

It was then only a 20-or-so minute stroll to the sleepy little town of Tagnag, which was essentially just a small collection of lodges built to service the track heading over the Cho La Pass. The snow was really coming down now, and by the time we arrived in Tagnag, I was a walking snowman.

'You is looking like the Yeti,' Subash said.

'Speak for yourself!'

We stood outside the lodge while Subash went inside to get a broom - the same one they sweep the floor with - came back outside and frantically started brooming the snow off me and Nima. I tried to swat him away but he was relentless. We then dived inside the warmth of the dining room and ordered many, many cups of tea.

I noticed with despair that the same, noisy group of Koreans from Namche Bazaar were in a corner playing some weird Korean board game, which involved the women grabbing the men's hands, holding them still, and then beating the shit out of them while they all noisily laughed. Even the men getting their hands belted were in hysterics. They were a strange people. I just hoped they were going to wear themselves out. I passed the afternoon drinking tea, wizzing heaps and having a chat with a pleasant Irishman that I had met in Nunthala, the night before I woke up sick. I had seen him again in Bupsa before he steamed off ahead.

The snow was relentless. Just before it got dark I went for a wander outside and noticed with a touch of apprehension that there was at least a foot of fresh snow on the ground. That was at 4700m and I wondered what it might look like at the Cho La Pass at a dizzying height of 5420 metres (17780ft).

I dined on a terribly bland version of Dal Bhat, reasoning that every single ingredient to make it had to be carried here on the back of a porter or yak. I called it a night at 8pm. Half of the Koreans were still making copious amounts of noise in the dining room, while the other half were clattering around upstairs. I put my headphones in and let the melodic voice of Jimmy Cliff send me to sleep.

Well the album only went for just over an hour. As soon as it went silent, the noise of the Koreans came into play. A symphony of slamming doors rudely pulled me from a deep slumber in which I was crossing lush, warm rivers in tropical places. *What is wrong with these people?* They did not have one considerate bone in their entire bodies. The man in the room next to me had cranked up a noisy, portable gas stove that hissed away without regulation, while his roommate was singing a Korean pop song so hideous that I began to wish I was hearing impaired. The lady across from me unlocked her door, opened it, slammed it, stomped down to the toilet door, opened it, slammed it, before repeating the process on the return trip.

I am not exaggerating here. This happened continuously until around 11pm, when the noise finally died down. However, because they ate and drank so much at dinner (no shit...they had five or six courses) they were up all night going to the toilet with the usual accompaniment of slammed doors and stomping feet. I just don't understand it. I had this conversation days ago with Juliet and Michael, and we were talking up the extent of our own consideration. We unlock our doors as gently as possible, make sure the doors don't slam, and then tip-toe down the wooden corridors to minimalize any form of noise. I even gently let one rip in the night lest it disturb the neighbours. Not these Koreans. They fart and carry on as if it is a competition. Bastards.

Then they all woke up at 3.30am. I thought they were going to tackle the pass early, but they were in fact still clattering around at 6.30am when everyone else left. They didn't wake up at 3.30am and think: *You know what, I bet that because it is 3.30am everyone else staying in this lodge is still sleeping, and so I will go about my business as quietly as possible.* Au contraire! More like: *I am a Korean wanker, and because I am awake, everyone must also be awake too!*

I entered the dining hall knowing that I looked ridiculously tired. The Koreans were all gathered around, having a nine-course meal. They all looked fresh and ready to tackle the pass. I could think of nothing I'd rather do less than wander into dangerously thin air across a pass more difficult than the first one. A pass I'd only just managed to cross after a rest day.

This one was a bit higher too, and it had been snowing for 10 hours the previous night.

'Morning man, you sleep well?' asked Subash as he entered the dining room.

'Does it look like I slept well?'

'Maybe nots.'

'Subash, we are not staying in the same place as those damn Koreans again,' I said, loud enough for the whole room to hear, although I don't believe they understood a word of English.

'Those damn Koreans!' said the Irishman as he walked into the hall, loud enough for the whole room to here. We were pissed off people. 'I barely slept a wink all night.'

I gave him a look that cried understanding, before going back to poking my rancid vegetable omelette around my plate with a fork. The Irishman had big plans on getting to Gokyo and exploring the sacred lakes, but he was so tired he was just looking forward to getting to Gokyo so he could have a lazy day.

Chapter Fourteen

TACKLING THE CHO LA PASS

It was bitterly cold when we left the lodge, a little after 6.30am. My poor little toes felt as though they were frozen to the inside of my boots. We let the Koreans go first so that they could break a trail through the fresh snow, punishment for being such a bunch of dick-heads. The track climbed steadily up along a pristine v-shaped valley, formed by a stream that somehow managed to flow despite the temperature being around the -10°C mark.

There was very little in the way of vegetation, but the fresh snow gave the air a clean, untouched feeling. As clear as only mountain air can be.

'What is wrong with you today?' asked Subash as he stopped for the fortieth time in half an hour to wait for me.

'What do you mean? Am I going slow?'

'I mean you are counting your steps today.'

I realised he was right. I was so tired and not in the right frame of mind for tackling one of the passes.

'I am exhausted man. I didn't sleep because of those damn Koreans.'

'Ok man no problems, just keep moving.'

We went up for a long time, although the gradient wasn't too ridiculous. The people that had set off before me had left decent tracks in the snow that acted as steps for my exhausted feet. As we rounded the top of a hill, Cho La came into sight for the first time. It looked daunting. And frustrating. We had dragged our arses up to 5200 metres above sea-level, but now we had to painfully surrender some of that precious altitude by heading back down into a wide, snow-filled gulley.

The pace-setters had all chosen this spot for a rest, so I plonked myself down and gorged on some chocolate, willing the sugar to give me something. Anything. Two of the porters began to play fight about 10-or-so metres away from me. Then they began to wrestle in the snow while the others egged them on, laughing and cheering wildly. Eventually one of them trapped the other's arm and put him in a submission hold, while the porter with his face in the snow began tapping the ground wildly. The winner looked at me as if for approval, as though I was a professional wrestler. It was all fun and games, but at this altitude it was very silly. On his way down the next slope, the winner fell heavily and slid down the icy slope for a good few metres. It took him a long time to get up, and then an even longer time to regather his load. He was the only porter I saw fall to such an extent in Nepal. He was clearly spent from the fight.

We went down and waded through waist-deep snow at the base of the gully, before heading back up. This time we were heading up to the pass. Then the ascent really began over loose rocks that moved underneath deep snow. Vertical walls of rock and ice rose all around us. Boulders the size of footballs dislodged themselves from unknown heights above us and entered free fall, landing with an almighty cracking sound – the sound of high-speed rock on rock. It was most disconcerting.

Then we hit a steep section, which perfectly coincided with the path turning to one solely of ice. It was very slippery and on a few occasions I would have been unable to climb higher unless Subash had pulled me up. God he was strong for a little fella. I negotiated the steep ice, but I was utterly buggered. I had a system, though. *Just five steps. Then you can have a rest. Just take five steps.* I'd take the five steps and gasp for breath while my thighs weakened and plotted against me. *Ok, five steps were too much. Just take four steps this time, then you can have a rest.* I was literally counting my steps now, but it was all I had. At least it kept me moving.

I knew how hard it was going to be this time. However, I thought I may have been slightly better acclimatised to this altitude after crossing the Renjo La, but it wasn't the case. I was locked in exactly the same epic battle of willpower with myself as I was a few days before.

I saw some people coming the other way. They had crossed the pass and were now on their way down, but there was something very unnatural in their movements. As they came closer, I realised that two or three men were dragging someone down the slope. Closer still I realised it was a Caucasian man, perhaps only 20 years old. He looked at me as they dragged him past. His head bounced off rocks, his face pealed as it scraped over ice, and his eyes lolled somewhere to the back of his head.

'We must keep moving!' Subash said anxiously, snapping me instantly from a state of utter confusion. I could hear something in his voice that I had not heard before. Was it panic? I knew I had been sitting in one spot for an abnormally long amount of time, but I simply did not have the strength to continue. 'Man this is a very dangerous places. You see all these rocks that are falling?'

'I see them, Subash, but there is nothing I can do. Sorry. I am too tired. I need to rest. Was that boy ok?'

'He has the altitude sickness. He will be ok if they get him down to a lower altitude in quick enough times. From Tagnag they will go to Gokyo and then call for helicopter. Come, I take your bag.'

'Ok, thanks mate. How far to top?'

'For me, seven minutes. For you maybe half-hour.'

I struggled upwards. Every breath became a war. It is not that there are actually fewer oxygen molecules at this altitude, but rather that the air pressure is so much less that the molecules are more thoroughly dispersed. Imagine at sea level there is an ocean of air above you, the weight of which compresses the oxygen molecules into a very dense structure, so there is far more oxygen to breathe in. Whatever the science, I just could not get enough of that vital essence.

I was now down to two-step rests. I put my head down and refused to look up at the pass. I didn't want to see it until I was there. My agony was directly proportionate to my determination to get to the top. The harder it became, the more I wanted to succeed. If I had to turn around, it was a long, long way back to Tagnag, and then to Gokyo, where we would have to wave white flags and stumble back to the Khumbu Highway via a different and far easier track.

'Oh Mr Gorong! Say "cheese"!' I heard Subash call. His voice was close. I looked up and he was sitting on a boulder only 20 metres higher than me, and began furiously snapping photos of me with my camera.

'Subash, is that the pass?' I gasped.

'Yes, is pass.'

'Don't bullshit me Subash. When I get to you, is there any more up?'

'Maybe only 5 metres of up.'

'Is the view good?'

'No. No good view from Cho La Pass.'

'What you mean no good view? You mean it is cloudy?'

'No. I is meaning you can't see a things from the Cho La. It is not like the Renjo La.'

I laughed out loud, paused to suck in some sparse oxygen molecules, then laughed again.

'Then why the hell did we come all the way up here?' I asked him.

'You tell me where you want to go, and I is guiding you there,' he answered simply and irrefutably. I laughed again, elated that I was almost there. One step, rest. One step, rest. Every inch I climbed took a monumental effort. It really is hard to fathom if you haven't been to that altitude before. Every step I took, Subash snapped a photo of me.

'Subash you're putting me off!' I cried.

'No,' he answered simply without removing his eye from the scope of my camera.

'Yes, you are!'

'Just come up man, and I stop.'

'You better hope you're not there when I get there,' I mumbled inaudibly and then carried on. I passed Subash who turned the camera around while I made my way ever-so slowly up the final 5 metres of rock. Then I simply collapsed, slumping onto the stone cairn dressed in prayer flags, while Subash was there to capture the moment immortally in the form of a very good photo. I was at 5420m, or 17782 feet for all you backward folk. I didn't stay on the pass too long. I didn't want to end up like that poor boy being dragged down.

A large amphitheatre-shaped cirque announced the beginning of the next valley, where snow accumulated in abundance, leading to the formation of an immense sheet of hard, blue ice. We climbed down a near-vertical section of rock and snow and then joined the path into the Khumbu region. Then I slipped and began sliding towards a gaping crevasse, but luckily I executed a spectacular starfish technique to arrest my fall. I slid for perhaps a metre and had Subash diving to grab my back. I was never really in danger due to the spectacular starfish technique, but had I gained speed on that ridiculously steep slope I may have disappeared without a trace into the guts of the mountain.

'Come on man, you want to fall into a crevasse?' Subash asked me as he helped drag me to my feet.

'Not really, didn't you see my technique?'

'I see you sliding towards a crevasse.'

I laughed, just relieved that I was still above ground. The path was perilous. It was less than a foot wide with a steep drop down onto the glacier on one side, the other a vertical wall housing a multitude of unstable-looking boulders. It would have been scary enough with fresh legs, let alone mine, which were weary and shaking. It was so narrow that you had to assume a tight-rope walker impression. We were late to the pass, and so clouds were beginning to swirl around the highest peaks, shielding the view. But it mattered not, for my eyes were firmly focused on the most dangerous and challenging part of the trek so far.

For about half an hour I slid and skidded in the deep snow, each time holding my breath and praying that I would not start sliding out of control. Then I'd pay for having held my breath and my lungs would begin to scream for air. I'd stand there in a state of hyperventilation until my lungs absorbed enough oxygen and my head began to clear. Slowly, the deep snow made way to a combination of snow and rocks large enough to protrude through to the surface.

I looked up and stared in wonder. There was Ama Dablam, cloaked in white, rising the highest of all the hundreds of peaks in the vicinity. It wasn't the traditional view of the mountain, the famous view in all the postcards, but was from an entirely different angle.

I had circumnavigated the mountain through a host of different valleys and gullies and now I was staring straight at the western wall of this grand monolith. An eagle soared high above, then swooped down and began circling us. *He's waiting for me to 'carc it'* (from 'carcass', meaning to die!), I thought, and then snapped some beautiful pictures of this beautiful mountain. It was miles and miles away, but also right there. Almost near enough to touch. I sat down, exhausted. Nima thrust a packet of chocolate biscuits into my hand and I ate one before trying to give it back to him. He was having none of it.

'Eat, sir,' was all he said. Subash similarly would not accept them, so I ate a few more and put the rest in my pocket.

If I'd thought the hard part was over, I was sadly mistaken. Snow gave way to rock and ice, and lots of it. We scrambled down boulders the size of cars, some of them even moved at the touch, a most concerning realisation.

'Please don't kill me,' Subash said from below.

'Only if I don't kill myself first.'

I fell hard on several occasions. Everyone did. It was perhaps a little harsh, but when I saw one of the porters fall it made me feel pretty good. It wasn't just me. I think the only person that didn't fall was Nima, who was already a tiny speck nearing the bottom of the slope. How did he do it?

About three-quarters of the way down, the dreaded thing happened. I slipped on a vertical, icy drop, except that my right knee stayed where it was while the rest of me came crashing down. It twisted in a sickening way, and I felt all kinds of unnatural grinding and carrying on. The trip had been a bit of a risk from the very beginning as I was attempting it with a ruptured posterior cruciate ligament (PCL) in my right knee, remnants of an old rugby injury.

I lay there with my leg on the upwards slope, the rest of me sitting in a pool of water between two jagged rocks. I dared not move. I looked around to see if anyone had seen me fall (funny the things I sometimes worry about). Subash was too far ahead, and I was shielded from the porters above me by an over-hanging cliff-face. I moved my knee slowly, bending it to see the extent of the damage. It was sore, but I didn't think it was damaged (any more than it already was).

I stood on it slowly, and at first, it was as though someone had jabbed a knife straight into the side. I took the weight off of it and tried again with the same reaction, only this time it wasn't as bad. Standing on my left leg I reached for my bag and had a gulp of water. I tried again. This time it was just sore, with no shooting pains. *Well thank God for that!*

I carried on, as cautious as ever, and somehow managed to negotiate that awful section of rock without too much more drama. The rocks turned to dirt, which I didn't mind sliding down on my arse. And then something remarkable happened. We joined the valley floor and it was *flat*. I'm not talking Nepali flat. This was Australian flat. It was wonderful. For perhaps 3 kilometres we walked on flat, flat ground, the only obstacle being about six inches of snow; but the trekkers that headed the other way in the morning had left us the perfect path. I had a sore knee and a slight limp, but I was having fun again.

After another half an hour we came to a bit of a rise. Not much, but it was a testament to how much the pass had taken out of me that even the slightest ascent almost brought me to tears. It was really hard again. We weren't climbing up a mountain, but more of a gigantic mound on the middle of the valley floor. It may have even been terminal moraine if you want to talk technical. It took close to 20 minutes with me doing the '10 step equals 10 second break' routine before we came over a gentle rise and saw the tiny town of Dzong La nestled on another area of flat ground. Subash took off ahead, I assumed to get my room sorted for when I eventually stumbled in. Once I finally joined him he said, 'Ok man, Koreans staying in the other one tonight, we staying in this one. No one going to disturb you tonight.'

I could have hugged him.

I flopped into the lodge, banging my head in the process on the door frame that stood only four feet from the ground. I ordered a pot of masala tea, which was the nicest thing I've ever drank, even with my nose dripping into the cup. Two other men were in the dining room.

They were kitted out in Korean beanies, with Korean patches sewn onto their jackets and trousers. They were dressed exactly the same as the 'other' Koreans. I panicked at first, but as I walked in they bowed to me and didn't say a word. They were different. I calmed down instantly.

They turned out to be mountain climbers, immediately obvious from their boots. They were climbing Choletse (6440m, 21128ft), the mountain right next to us, and were using this lodge as their base camp, 4800m above sea level. They didn't make a peep all night. I wished them luck as we walked out of camp the next morning, and not really understanding me, they just said 'Namaste!' and bowed their heads once more. I apologised in my head for stereotyping all Koreans as noisy and self-centred, and stepped out into the fresh morning snow, headed for Everest Base Camp.

Chapter Fifteen

TO GORAK SHEP AND A CHANGE OF PLANS

A few things happened this morning that were to shape the rest of the trip. First of all, Subash realised that we needed to steam roll ahead to stay on schedule. We were meant to get to EBC that day and shoot back down to Gorak Shep to spend the night. The following morning was the steep and draining climb of Kallar Pathar to get a glimpse of Everest, before heading back to Lobuche to sleep in preparation for the third pass the following morning, the somewhat scary Kongma La. After that we'd have to put in some long days in order to get all the way back to

Lukla on the 26th of March for our flight back to Kathmandu.

What immediately became obvious that morning was that I was very tired from the pass the day before. Nay, I was exhausted. It was a fairly easy ramble to Lobuche, but by the time we arrived I could barely take another step, let alone climb up to Base Camp that same day. Subash had been setting a real hot pace all morning, and I simply could not keep up. In the end I got a bit fed up of him, and just dropped off the pace, walking at my own speed. I found myself all alone for long periods of time. Except I wasn't entirely alone. I had Ama Dablam and Cholotse for company. I had them all to myself. You could do far worse.

We climbed high before joining the main Everest Base Camp path, and once again I expected to see a long trail of people training to see Everest, but I was once again impressed to see nothing but snow and mountains for as far as the eye could see. I was blessed with my first glimpse of Pumori, standing majestically at the end of yet another valley. We walked down to connect with the path, which stood over the other side of a great snowfield that we duly wandered across.

As we joined the main path we were passed by perhaps a dozen trekkers heading in the opposite direction. I was, as usual, just wearing a short-sleeved t-shirt; and as usual I was over-heating. I am a hairy man, so I had a built-in down-jacket. I passed two weird-looking German girls, one of whom said, 'Ooooh tough man!' In quite a weird German voice. I didn't know if she was being sarcastic or not, and I was of course way too tired to find out.

We strolled into the little village of Lobuche, essentially a collection of lodges and shops. Lobuche could adequately be described by the two words 'shit pit', which is a shame because its situation is breath-taking, nestled between some of the greatest mountains in existence. Lobuche Peak rises dramatically behind the town, while Nuptse dominates the other side of the valley. Yet here was Lobuche, crap everywhere and filthy. I stepped into an empty, wooden dining hall with typical expedition-based memorabilia plastered on every visible surface and ordered a bowl of noodle soup. I sat there, kind of dumbfounded that I was no longer walking. It felt like I'd been on the go for days without rest.

'Subash I think we're gonna have to rethink the schedule,' I said.

'You is looking the very tired.'

'26 days to do the pass, I think no way. Not with being sick and an extra acclimatisation day.'

'Ok so we take 28 days, have an extra rest day in Lobuche, then go over pass.'

'We'd have to re-arrange the flights then.'

'Man this is a no problems. This is my a job.'

'The problem is that only gives me a day and a half to explore Kathmandu and the valley. I wanted longer than that,' I pondered.

'What you want me do?' he asked, a little exasperated.

I thought for a second then said, 'Nothing. Don't do anything. Let me eat my noodles and drink my tea, then I'll tell you.'

All I could think about was the Cho La pass. How lucky we were to get across it. Less than a week before we tackled it, it was closed, and I could see why. The snow was treacherously deep in parts, particularly on the upper, steeper slopes. I'm no expert, but the whole situation cried 'avalanche' to me. Combine that with the rock falls on the other side of the pass walls, and I'd say it was not altogether a safe climb. But I had to get back to the schedule. What was I going to do? Something had to give.

'So you reckon this Kongma La Pass is harder and more dangerous than Cho La?' I asked.

'Yes of course,' Subash answered, but then he uncharacteristically stared at the ground. Even the mention of Kongma La brought about a change in the guides. They'd immediately stop speaking English, but would converse in their own tongue, in hushed voices and urgent whispers. It scared them. 'Kongma La only just open. Much snow up there and because it's 5535 metres and this time of years, the snow is freezing on loose rocks. This is a dangerous pass now.'

'Ok where's your map Subash?' he fumbled around in his bag for a minute, then rolled it out on the table before us. 'Ok so we're here, and we stay here tonight. Then Everest Base Camp tomorrow morning, but how are we going for time if we miss the Kongma La pass?'

'Man this is your destinies. You must go over the pass.'

'Two things mate. First is that I went over Renjo La and Cho La, both after rest days and both times I only just got over. Now you want to take me over the hardest one without a rest day? I don't think I'd be able to do it. Second, this isn't my destiny. To climb over a pile of rocks. I have been doing that for 23 days now. I am not that ambitious or goal orientated like some people, who would consider it a failure of a trip if they didn't climb something they said they were going to climb. So don't feel bad man, because I don't. And you said there was nothing to see up there right?'

'Yes there is no good views from there, no. Only glacier. Good view from Renjo La, but no Kongma La.'

'Sorted. It's good too because I'll get to see some of the villages from the Everest Base Camp trek that I wouldn't have seen otherwise.'

It was amazing. The mood immediately lightened and Subash and Nima went back to being their normal selves. They were relieved. We hadn't heard of or met anyone that had been over the Kongma La this season, which is unusual because we met heaps of people tackling the other two passes. Subash told me afterwards he was very worried about breaking a new trail on that pass.

We went and sat upstairs in the sunroom that doubled as some kind of weird waiting room for a couple of leaking loos. It was awkward when we'd be sitting there, keeping warm with the sun's rays streaming in through the large, glass windows, and someone would stroll down the corridor and give us a mortified look because we were sitting metres from a toilet separated from the room only by a thin, rickety old door with a coat-hanger for a lock. They'd enter, and we'd politely listen to all the accompanying noises while pretending we hadn't heard a thing. Nima sprawled himself out and was immediately in a coma.

'Nima is really tired,' I said while snapping a multitude of photos of the sleeping Sherpa.

'Yes of course, we is all a tireds,' Subash answered.

'Really?' I asked, unsure if he was being serious.

'Yes man!' he shouted, a little unexpectedly. 'Of course, we been trekking for more than 3 weeks.'

I guess I had just viewed Subash and Nima as superhuman. Their strength in times of adversity was just mind boggling to me. I would not have made it very far without them, I can assure you now.

A group of Estonians flooded the little dunny foyer and the room became uncomfortably crowded. At one stage Subash announced he was leaving, but a big eastern European hand was placed firmly on his shoulder and the thickly accented voice of the owner said, 'Sit, sit, no problem. Soon we go shopping and leave you in peace.'

Shopping in Lobuche. Very funny. Subash was swayed by the man, but I was having none of it, so I retired to my shit hole of a room, climbed into bed and went to sleep. I was out for a good two hours before I awoke, realised I was still in Lobuche, sighed, then went back to sleep again. When I finally awoke, it was to little knocks on the door, and I could hear Nima's voice whispering that I should come downstairs for dinner. I went, ate a disgusting bowl of spaghetti, which was just spaghetti and tomato ketchup that had been diluted with water. It was vile, but I ate it, needing the carbs. I then drank a delicious cup of ginger, lemon and honey tea (or maybe it was just delicious because everything else was a let-down) and then went back to my room and wrote until my laptop ran out of battery. I folded it and put it away, turned off my little two-watt light and went to bed once more.

We were high now. About 4900m above sea level, and it really began to show. I'd wake in the night and be gasping for air as my breathing naturally slowed down. Even when I wasn't gasping for air, I just couldn't gain any continuity with my sleeping. It was 20 minutes on, wake up, lay there for a while, go back to sleep, repeat. And so I passed the night. It was really cold too. Just thought I'd throw that in there. It is hard to sleep when you can't expose a single body part to the cold, because if you do, the cold lets you know about it very quickly.

*

Do you ever struggle to sleep all night, and then as soon as the sun begins to come up you just conk out? Well that's what happened to me in Lobuche and I awoke, yet again, with soft Nima taps at the door imploring me to come downstairs for breakfast. And that's all the mention that breakfast gets I'm afraid. It looked like dog shit and quite frankly that probably would have been an improvement. I drank an entire large pot of tea instead, packed my bag incredibly slowly, gasped for breath as I shoved my sleeping bag away, then just kind of sat at the end of my bed, a little deflated, just waiting for the inevitable arrival of Nima to collect my bag.

I hadn't even put my boots on yet. They were literally frozen solid and it didn't look like much fun. I could have sat there all day in a state of bliss, but I knew we had to keep on moving. It was Base Camp day, and I should have been enthused, but I just could not recover at this altitude. Nima showed up and I was forced into action. I cursed as I put my feet into the freezer that was my boots, attempted to lace them up, failed to get them anywhere near tight enough, and with boots rubbing at the heal I got up and trudged downstairs into a less than impressive hazy day.

The going from Lobuche was pretty steady. We weren't out to break any land speed records after all. At first the ground slanted up, but ever so slightly, almost imperceptibly. What was, however, entirely perceptible was the lack of oxygen, which made itself abundantly clear after only a few steps on flat ground. So I plodded, and plodded well. We made pretty good time. After a while Nuptse began to really increase in size in our right-hand flank, while Pumori shrank below a mound of moraine. Then we were standing at the foot of that moraine, and the path went straight up it. *This is going to be hard,* I thought, and guessed correctly. A few steps and I was buggered. I looked up and saw, of all people, the Koreans just ahead of me. Not the nice, quiet Koreans, but my mortal enemies. Wow, they were struggling. More than me. Their pain gave me strength and I powered past them, flicked my beard in the breeze while the sparkle of the sun glinted from my eyes, and then I raised my middle finger.

Of course the exertion to get past them left me light-headed and delirious. I struggled up and up despite it being the most mediocre of hills. When eventually on top I collapsed on a rock and gulped for air. Once I'd had enough of that I gulped at my water bottle to remove my tongue from the roof of my mouth after it had assumed a super-glue impression. Then I gulped for air once more, paying the price for not breathing while drinking. I stared at Subash and he stared back. We were both breathless.

Too much talking and no makes it, he seemed to say to me. So silently I stood, nodded, hoisted my pack and hauled my heavy arse slowly forwards. The Koreans had just taken the hill and looked at me with wonder as I carried on walking and they collapsed on rocks and struggled for air and water. We carried on up through the moraine. It was a lot of up and down on a thin trail of loose dirt and rocks, but mostly it was up. We did have a few hundred metres to ascend to the last village, Gorak Shep. I synced my breathing with my feet - one breath, one step, breathe out, another step. Repeat. It was unreal that so much breathing was required for such a small output of work. One breath, a very deep diaphragm-inducing breath, and all I had to show for it was two steps at barely a metre. At least it was comfortable and it allowed me to poke along the track.

After an hour or so we climbed up onto a bit of lateral moraine higher than anywhere else on the track, and standing before us was the Khumbu Glacier in all its glory, smashing and grinding its way down the valley. It was different, the Khumbu Glacier. All the others that I had seen were pig-ugly masses of dirty, black ice, but this one, formed at the knees of Everest herself, was clean and white and reflected the sun so efficiently that it was impossible to stare at it without sunglasses on. At the base of a large rock buttress, and indeed scattered over more stable parts of the glacier, were tiny yellow and orange tents. They were far away, probably another 5-6 kilometres as the crow flies, but I knew immediately what I'd seen. Everest Base Camp. The end of the track.

I struggled on and was eventually overtaken by the Estonian crew.

'See this man?' asked Subash's mate from the day before. 'He is superman.'

'Superman, really?' I wanted to know.

'Yes he is 75 years old.'

And he was overtaking me with a full pack on his back. Bravo, sir. The bloke looked about 60.

I vowed not to let him out of my sight, and spent the rest of the walk to Gorak Shep tailing the man of steel. We took great care to descend the final track into Gorak Shep. It was probably only a vertical 30m drop, but snow from the night before was somewhat incredulously beginning to melt and it was quite slippery. We strolled along flat ground into a lodge, which shall remain nameless, solely because Subash assured me that all the lodges were equally as shit as each other, and my mum always used to say, *'If you don't have anything nice to say, don't say anything at all.'*

It had taken us two and a half hours. Not bad really. I innocently ordered the mixed fried noodles and a small pot of milk tea, and sat down in the surreally warm room, plastered like never before with expedition and trekking group memorabilia. People from Spain, Brazil, Bahrain, Saudi Arabia, England, Portugal, Korea, Japan, Australia and Uruguay had all left something behind, and that was only in the small corner I was sitting in. The tea arrived and I added a metric tonne of sugar and sipped at the mountain elixir, feeling my strength returning by the minute. It is hard to mess up tea.

Then the noodles arrived. Ok, a word of warning. Don't order mixed fried noodles in the far reaches of the Nepali Himalaya.

'What the fuck is that?' I stared down at what had been put in front of me.

'This is the mixed noodles man,' Subash kindly informed me.

'I can see that, but what is *mixed* in it?'

'Everythings,' he answered. 'Noodles, vegetable, egg, cheese, and tunas.'

'And tunas?'

'Yes man and the tunas! You is ordering the mixed.'

'If I'd known tuna and cheese were mixed into my stir-fry then I wouldn't have ordered mixed fried noodles!'

'Everywhere same!' he said.

'I hope this tuna is in a can, man. We are a long way from the ocean.'

'Yes, sames.'

I looked at him blankly, then returned to the plate. It was bloody huge! The biggest meal I'd yet had. I could see Mt Everest staring at me from a chunk of tuna. There was Lhotse next to it. I dug my fork into the repulsive mixture and stared in horror as a bit of tuna jelly wobbled over a bit of fried egg. Then I gagged. I had to try it. I was making a bit of a scene and people were starting to look at me. I put the fork in my mouth and was immediately knocked in the head with a sledge hammer made of cheese. It was like someone had put a snooker ball inside a filthy trekking sock and then smacked me right on the tongue.

"Heeeeblur..." I made a noise.

"HEBLUUUR!" Another one, but louder. Then I spat into my napkin as a third noise was bringing with it stuff from deep down. Subash looked at me with concern. I'd eaten absolutely everything put in front of me this trip, but this was not food. They were trying to poison me.

'It's ok man, just the altitude,' said Subash.

I wanted to donk him on the head with the teapot I was now holding, pouring more tea to get rid of that God-awful flavour.

'If you can't eat no problems man,' Subash said. 'You maybe is making yourself a sicks.'

'I can't eat it!' I cried, my eyes watering from gagging.

A menu was shoved in front of me and I cringed. I ordered plain fried rice. I looked across and Nima was getting stuck in to that revolting dish. I've owned dogs that wouldn't have gone near that. As a poor porter, he could not afford to eat such delicacies as tuna and egg this high up in the mountains. The meal cost about $6.

The fried rice came. As a formula it would look something like this: $x = $ revolting $-$ tuna $+$ egg. I poked at it for a bit, stuffed a few meagre-sized bites in my mouth and then shoved it towards Nima. He ate the whole lot, two of my meals on his own. What a guy.

'So man shall we go to Base Camp?' Subash enquired, although he was a little coy. I think he was expecting me to get angry.

'Yes anywhere but Gorak bloody Shep,' I said as we walked out.

Chapter Sixteen

EVEREST BASE CAMP

I went up to my room and dumped everything out of my bag save the camera and a bottle of water. The smallest bed I had ever seen was crammed into the smallest room I had ever seen. An Umpa Lumpa would have been claustrophobic in this space. The bed had been cut in half to accommodate the opening and closing of the door.

'Its ok, sir?' asked Nima, knowing that it wasn't.

'It'll do!' I sighed, then walked out.

'Man hard to find the single rooms in Gorak Shep,' said Subash when I came downstairs. He knew I'd seen the room.

'No problem! Have I ever complained? Let's go to Base Camp.'

The track was mercifully level at first. It was just like walking, except with the accompanying breathing difficulties at 5180m above sea level. After a good 15 minutes we hit the moraine again and began the up and down motion of the morning climb. We joined a steep cliff face, peppered with boulders of dubious stability. Dubious enough to have me quicken my pace. At times the sharp sound of rock-on-rock echoed off distant walls and we'd pause and look around, trying to ascertain if we were about to be in the firing line. We climbed away from the steep cliff face and joined a ridge of lateral moraine positioned about 100 metres from the base of the valley wall, and once we were at the top, the ridge mercifully flattened off. In fact, it flattened off for a long way, and Base Camp re-emerged into view, but this time much, much closer.

Two people were coming the opposite way. One was undoubtedly a guide, but he was supporting the weight of the second person who could barely walk. Together, painfully slowly, they made their way back towards Gorak Shep.

'Subash can you please ask them if they're ok?'

'Yes man.'

He blurted out the question in Nepali to the guide, who seemed a little bit confronted by the enquiry. It was as though we had questioned his honour.

'He said no problems. That she is just a little dizzy from altitude.'

'She looked more than a little dizzy,' I said.

'Yes, but sometimes the guides is a crazy. They is a pushes and pushes to getting the clients to Base Camp, now she is getting the mountain sickness. She needs a helicopter.'

'Can we do anything to help her?' I asked, and he sensed my urgency.

'No man. First things is they slowly go back to Gorak Shep then is calling the helicopter.'

'Ok,' I reluctantly replied. It just seemed such an un-Australian thing to do, to let those people struggle all the way back to the next town, when we were there and could help them. I reminded myself that we weren't in Australia and that I'd essentially been told to drop it, and so I turned my back on the struggling girl and guide and carried on the path to Base Camp.

Nuptse had followed us all the way up the valley. It really was a magnificent-looking mountain. As we walked it continually changed form, and it seemed to become more impressive with every step that we took. Its long, ridge-like top is crowned by seven summits, ranging from 7861m down to 7695m, but as its topographic prominence is a mere 319m, it does not actually feature on the list of highest mountains. I think that is a terrible shame. I had a real fascination with Nuptse. When viewed from Lobuche or indeed any place between there and Base Camp, what you see is a real, spectacular and ever-changing mountain. On occasion the clouds being violently blown around the summit cleared just enough for Everest to poke its tiny black face through, before disappearing moments later.

I looked up at Mount Everest, much closer now, as large, fluffy snow-flakes began drifting over my shoulder from the opposite direction. I craned my neck until it hurt. Up there, some of the most famous explorers ever to have graced this earth had lost their lives. I thought, specifically, of George Mallory and Sandy Irvine, who were last seen alive by human eyes in 1924, before they disappeared into a cloud. The pair of eyes belonged to one Noel Odell, who had this report of the event:

'At 12.50, just after I had emerged from a state of jubilation at finding the first definite fossils on Everest, there was a sudden clearing of the atmosphere, and the entire summit ridge and final peak of Everest were unveiled. My eyes became fixed on one tiny black spot silhouetted on a small snow-crest beneath a rock-step in the ridge; the black spot moved. Another black spot became apparent and moved up the snow to join the other on the crest. The first then approached the great rock-step and shortly emerged at the top; the second did likewise. Then the whole fascinating vision vanished, enveloped in cloud once more.'

Odell stated with some degree of certainty that the pair were 'going strong for the top', but by the time the clouds cleared, all traces of the two had vanished under a blanket of snow and ice. Debate has raged for years over whether or not Irvine and Mallory were the first climbers to summit Everest, and even the man himself, Sir Edmund Hillary, contested to searching for traces of the climbers when he reached those heights on the first-ever successful summit in 1953.

Mallory's body wasn't found until 1999, when legendary mountain and rock climber

Conrad Anker stumbled upon it. The party searched for the mountaineer's camera, but it was one of the few things missing from the inventory, perhaps the only thing that could have proved they were the first to summit, and then perished on the descent. Perhaps it was in the hands of Sandy Irvine, whose body remains missing until this very day. No one knows. Perhaps in a few decades, history as we know it will be rewritten. No one can say.

I looked up and thought of the people that had their lives extinguished in the great climbing disaster of 1996. Everest seemed to take the shape of a tombstone. The largest tombstone in the world. Their bodies were still up there, scattered around the place like chicken feed, the effort and logistics required to remove them an unfeasible prospect. And then the clouds that were politely dusting us with snow continued their north-easterly journey and Everest vanished, along with the illusion.

Now I'd like to lighten the mood. I would like to tell you the story of a man named Maurice Wilson. It ultimately ends with his death on the high slopes of Mount Everest in 1934, but unlike his predecessors and his progenies, if you will, I think the conclusion to his story was *meant* to be on these slopes. Go make yourself a cup of tea, because it is a cracker!

Mr Maurice Wilson, or *Mozza* as he will henceforth be known, was born in Bradford in 1898 and was thrown into the family textile business. However, the Great War called him to the East and he enlisted in the army, where he became somewhat of a hero. During the Fourth Battle of Ypres, he was commanding a machine gun post that came under severe pressure from the German lines. The positions either side of him fell, everyone around him fell, his soldiers and fellow officers. Everyone. Yet our hero kept his head down, the Allies launched a counter-attack, and Mozza walked away from the incident with barely a scratch. The *London Gazette* reported that 'It was owing to his pluck and determination in holding his post that the enemy attack was held up.'

Mozza was awarded the Military Cross for his bravery, but before he could receive his award he was near-fatally wounded by machine-gun fire that tore into his left arm and chest. This happened while he was leading an Allied counter-attack.

So that's the kind of man we are dealing with in this story. A bloody legend.

He spent the next few years of his life travelling around the world in an unsettled kind of way. He made his way to New York, before leaving to New Zealand from San Francisco. Eventually he returned to England, but before long he became terribly ill. And then he disappeared. The only note he left for worried friends read: 'I must shake this thing off. If I come back you'll know that I am all right. If you don't see me again you'll know that I am dead.'

Not a great deal is known about where Mozza went and what he did. The little that we do know is that he did not take his illness to a doctor, but to a spiritual man that claimed to be able to cure all sicknesses. This man advised Mozza to fast for 35 days, only allowing small amounts of water into the body. After the fasting period, he told him to pray to God that he may be born again. And to Mozza, it was so.

While recovering, he came across, quite by accident, a newspaper clipping of the aforementioned 1924 expedition to Everest that saw Mallory and Irvine meet their makers. It planted a seed in his head. He knew that fasting and faith had saved his life. He *knew* that fasting and faith would be enough for him to do anything he set his mind to. And to prove it to the world, he said he would climb Mount Everest all by himself. So our mate Mozza conjured the greatest plan ever devised by a human being. He would crash-land a plane on the lower slopes of Everest and then be the first person to climb to the highest point on earth. The fact that he was neither a pilot, nor a mountaineer, didn't seem to bother him.

His training consisted of taking long, long walks. He was a demonic walker. He often walked from London to Bradford, a distance of 315km (195 miles) in less than five days. He walked in the Lake District and in the Welsh mountains, but at no point did he ever decide to grasp even the most fundamental basics of mountaineering. He purchased a 1930 Gipsy Moth, a two-seater aeroplane, and then named it Ever-Wrest. He learned to fly, but was an atrocious pilot. As his departure date loomed, Mozza decided to fly north to Bradford to bid his family farewell. And he almost made it. On his final approach, his engines spluttered and then died altogether, while he desperately tried to bring the diving aircraft under control. With less than a 1000 feet to spare, he brought Ever Wrest under control, spotted a field littered with a dozen cattle and attempted to land on the soft grass. Naturally, he got it all wrong, undershot the field and shredded his way through a waiting hedge. The plane flipped, leaving Mozza hanging upside down, the only thing preventing him from being dumped on his head was his seat belt. The story goes that he was found by a small boy, who helped him down and within minutes a Press photographer had arrived and the newspapers the following day had pictures of Mozza's proud face plastered over the front covers.

When his plane was fixed and ready to go once more, Wilson received a letter from the deputy director of Civil Aviation instructing him that flying over Nepal was strictly prohibited unless prior permission from the Nepalese government was first obtained, a step, they assured him, that was highly unlikely.

'I'm going on as planned,' he informed reporters that were following his story. 'Stop me? They haven't got a chance!'

He received a telegram forbidding him to take off from British shores, but he tore it up and boarded his one-man plan and hit the runway. A decent-sized group of both friends and reporters had gathered to witness the occasion, but to their utter horror Mozza had forgotten one of the most basic rules of flying a plane. He took off with the wind at his tail and he almost did not make it. Instead he reached the end of the runway and scampered over a patch of grass before rising inches above a hedge that waited like a spider's web at the perimeter of the airfield. He was off. Just.

First he flew to Freiburg in Germany and then Passau, over Lake Geneva to Marseilles, Pisa, Rome, Naples, across the Mediterranean Sea to Tunisia. An incident with the local police dictated a need to refuel himself from some rusty, old tanks, but unfortunately for Mozza, there was water in the fuel. He experienced engine trouble, yet as the engine started to splutter and die, he was able to make an emergency landing in Libya. With the problem solved, he continued to Tripoli, Benghazi, Tobruk, Sidi Barrani, Alexandria and Cairo. It had taken him seven days, but he was right on time.

He departed for Suez, Gaza, Bethlehem and Gadda, before arriving in Baghdad. All the while he was being hassled by the British government, who had 'misplaced' his permits to fly across Persia. So Mozza found a different way. He flew to Bahrain with the intention of making the epic journey across the Arabian sea via Sharjah in the UAE. The British government refused Mozza's request to refuel after arriving in Bahrain, and told him they would not allow him to fly to India. So Mozza promised them he'd backtrack to Baghdad. They fuelled him up and he took off, heading east for India. I like to imagine him holding up his finger as Bahrain decreased in size, with a wry smile on his face.

In Ruth Hanson's excellent biography of the man himself, *Maurice Wilson: A Yorkshireman on Everest*, she puts his achievement into perspective quite nicely;

'The little Gypsy Moth had carried him safely over 5000 precarious miles (8047km); she had been pushed to the limit in extreme temperatures and with variable fuel, but through all the cramped, lonely and wearing hours of concentrating, and listening for any change in the steady sound of her engine, Ever Wrest had kept going.'

Mozza sold his plane having been denied permission to fly over Nepali airspace, and took a train to Tibet, where he began his assault on the mountain.

And he gave it a bloody good shot too. Maurice Wilson died at 23000 feet above sea level, a little over 7000 metres. What he accomplished in flying that far would have been an outstanding achievement for an experienced, seasoned pilot, let alone a complete amateur with limited ability. He was an outstanding navigator, relying on maps (often really bad ones) and compasses to get him to his destination; even though some of the flights were right at the extent of Ever Wrest's flying range, and that getting lost even for 10 minutes could have meant the difference between life and death. He wasn't a mountaineer, but he climbed to a height of over 7000m, about the height of the 120th highest mountain in the world. He did it by himself.

*

The ridge of moraine we were traversing once again joined the steep valley wall, and once again I was left to nervously glance upwards to see the biggest boulders hung hazardously on a surface comprised of loose dirt and pebbles. Everywhere rocks, some the size of bowling balls, came crashing down to rest on our (yes, our!) walking track. It was most disconcerting.

'Subash, does this look a little dangerous to you?' I asked.

'Yes,' he answered, looking up. 'One day these rocks will kill some the groups.'

'You think?'

'Yes I know. Don't worry man, you is hiring me so safe.'

'What you gonna do, tackle me out of the way if one comes hurtling down?'

'Yes,' he replied matter-of-factly, turned and carried on walking.

'Awesome,' I muttered to myself and followed him within tackling distance. I then had visions of him trying to tackle me, little Subash, half my size, and me instinctively palming him off like you do in a game of rugby. Oops. Splat!

The ridge abruptly ended and we climbed down over a scree field with a barely discernible path. At one stage Subash called out to another guide leading the group of Estonians, who had inadvertently taken a wrong turn and was now leading the group towards an awkward section of exposed glacial ice. It was obvious from our lofty position, but down there it was a different story altogether. Realising his error, the guide called out a quick thank you and then altered his course accordingly.

'The path to Base Camp change every year. Every year, Base Camp change the places. Just dependings on what the glacier is a doing,' Subash told me and I nodded.

After climbing down, we cruelly had to climb up again. My knee was doing a weird clicking thing that made me anxious, especially seeing as the going was so rough and uneven. But it wasn't long before we were there. I saw

Subash take a couple of long steps. It looked like he was walking on flat ground. He was walking on flat ground! The things you get excited about at high altitude! I joined him and was greeted by the group of Estonians congratulating themselves in the form of a big group hug. Behind them a large and untidy stone cairn was wrapped in old, decaying prayer flags. Beyond that was a lunar landscape littered with bright-coloured tents.

I sat on a large rock and traced the route of the arresting Khumbu Glacier, the beginning of the ascent of Mount Everest. The ice was brilliantly clean. Without sun-glasses I was unable to stare at it for more than a few seconds. We sat in the middle of the most spectacularly desolate amphitheatre I had ever seen, with walls of rock and ice rising dramatically all around us. It would have been entirely gloomy save for a slither of daylight down the valley, the way that we had come from.

I looked upon Base Camp and the people strewn around the place. These people would be here for weeks, acclimatising and getting themselves ultra-fit before waiting for that small window of opportunity, and then they'd risk everything to get to the top. I understand professional mountaineers doing it, but not these client types that pay huge amounts of money to be guided to the top.

With the exception of 1977, people have died every year climbing Mount Everest from 1969-2013. Since 1970, 220 have perished attempting to reach the summit. That is a lot of people to leave behind. I'm not really going to join the great mountaineering debate, but it does just strike me as a bit of a selfish thing to do; risking your life to climb a mountain, particularly if you're an amateur.

Mount Everest wasn't climbed until 1953 for a good reason. It is among the most inhospitable places on our planet and we are not meant to be there. If you took someone from sea-level, picked them up and plopped them on top of Mt Everest, they'd enjoy the view for a few seconds before promptly passing out. Then they would die. 10 people gave their lives away in 2012, nine in 2013, 19 in 2014, most of whom died in a single avalanche (or ice fall). On the 25th of April, 2015, at least 22 people were killed when the 7.8 magnitude earthquake struck Nepal, after an avalanche thundered down the slopes of Pumori and in to Base Camp.

It is not getting any safer. I looked at all those people at Base Camp and I felt sorry for them. Some would have less than a month to live.

So with that sobering thought I snapped some pictures and we headed back the way we had come. The long climb down into the Base Camp basin meant a dangerous and sapping climb back up to the flat ridgeline past the dicey-looking boulders. I'm not going to say it was an easy hike back to Gorak Shep – nothing was easy at that altitude – but I will say that it was a lot easier. Faster too. It had taken close to two hours to get to Base Camp, but our return journey only set us back a little over an hour.

As we joined that flat section immediately before the village, we came across the guide and girl, still struggling back to Gorak Shep. At least they'd almost made it. I motioned to Subash that he should ask them if they wanted help again, which he did, and received the same response. Both guide and girl had a balaclava-type setup, so I did not really get to see what either of them looked like.

The closer we came, the faster Subash went until eventually I let him have it and began a nice relaxing stroll back to the Lodge. I was in no real rush to get there. There was nothing to do. My laptop battery was flat with no real hope of charging it. I wasn't looking forward to dinner. I wasn't too excited about going to sleep in a bed built for a Barbie doll. So I sat outside the front of the lodge for a good long time, looking up at Kallar Pathar, a big mound of rock offering excellent views of Mount Everest, which we were due to climb in the morning.

I couldn't say I was looking forward to it. I was exhausted. Behind it, Pumori rose sharply and disappeared in vast swirls of cloud. It began to snow. I watched as the guide and girl made it back to the lodge. The guide cleaned the mud off his boots on the cobblestone pavement and I watched as the girl made a feeble, uncoordinated attempt to do the same. She almost fell over and so gave it up and stumbled inside. I felt terribly sorry for her. Subash had another word with the guide, who told him that there was a helicopter coming for her tomorrow morning. *It could be too late by the morning,* I thought.

I realised they had Wi-Fi at the Lodge, so armed with some battery on my iPod I logged on and let the world know I was still alive. The wifi worked intermittently and cost so much I'll have to sell my car when I get home. Gorak Shep is a real bastard of a place. I hope you're picking up what I'm putting down.

I dined on fried potatoes, cooked with turmeric. They tasted like potatoes and turmeric. I put a big dollop of tomato ketchup on the side of my plate and dipped a big potato greedily in. Well I should have tried the ketchup first, because it was off. Who knows how long they'd had it for. It was rancid. Not for the first time that day I dived for the napkin and spat out my food. I sacrificed my knife to scrape the ketchup and the defiled potatoes even further to the side. I picked up the salt and poured a little bit onto my hand and licked. It tasted a little bit like salt, so I used plenty of that to mask the insipidity of the dish.

I was sat next to a Chinese man about my age with a friendly, approachable, babyish kind of face. We spoke for a little while, but his English was limited and my Chinese non-existent. I watched as his food was placed in front of him. He'd ordered chicken soup and a plate of fried rice. He was about to have a bite when his guide leaned across both Subash and myself, moved his bowl of soup about a foot across the table, then moved his plate a few inches before moving both the bowl and the plate back to where they had been in the first place. The Chinese man and myself looked at each other, raised our eyebrows and then burst out laughing. Sometimes they just want to be helpful when there is absolutely nothing for them to do (like when Nima brought me jam to go with my eggs).

The man dipped his spoon into his soup while I watched intently. He raised it to his lips and blew on it gently before draining the contents into his mouth. He then made a face as though he'd just bitten deep into a grapefruit, skin and all, then turned to me and said, 'Ahh no good.' He pushed the bowl of soup aside and commenced with the fried rice. I knew what it tasted like. I'd had two spoon-fulls for lunch and that was enough. Horrified that his bowl of soup was no longer in line with his plate, the guide lunged over me and Subash once more, and moved the bowl into five different locations so that his client would know the trouble he was going to, before moving it back in line. It was all very funny.

Despite the circumstances I went to bed a contented man. I had reached the most far-flung place of the trek and now I would be heading back towards civilisation minus a dangerous pass to tackle. It was mostly downhill, save for a tiring climb in the morning.

Chapter Seventeen

DOWNHILL

Sleep comes easily to few people at this altitude and it was the same for me. It was a long, long night. On the rare occasion that I did doze off, I'd be awoken by a great need for oxygen, and I'd find myself gasping for air. Another time my left leg, which was dangling over the cut-off edge of the bed, had gone completely numb as my blood circulation had been cut short. I had to get up and dance on it for a few minutes to revive it. Of course it was cold as well. It was the coldest place we stayed at. It was -9 degrees before I went to bed and that was only at 7pm. By 2am I was fed up. I grabbed my iPod, a book and my head lamp and disappeared under the covers for a few hours to see me through until dawn.

After what may have been the longest night of my life, I realised that dawn was slowly approaching. It was, however, far too cold to move anywhere. I didn't even have to expose myself to the air, just moving was enough to upset the warm equilibrium I had created for myself inside my sleeping bag. To move turned 20 degrees to -20 in one breathtaking instant. I glanced at my thermometer. It was -26 degrees. I'd agreed to meet Subash at 6am for the climb of Kallar Pathar, but when I found the energy to glance at my clock, that time was already long gone.

It was approaching half-past. I got up and layered up. It was a struggle. I threw on a fleece and a jacket and went to the toilet. En route, I looked out the window in the hallway and was confused not to see anything out the window apart from white. I went down the stairs and unlocked the front door. It was strange that I was so late up and yet I was the first one out the lodge. I opened the door and realised what was happening. It was snowing. It was a blizzard. *If you think I'm wasting valuable energy, Subash Gurung, to climb to a view point with no view, then how wrong you are!*

I trundled back to my room. I was relieved. I remembered joking with Subash the day before about how I might send him up Kallar Pathar with my camera to snap some photos. Now we'd both be saved the exertion.

I fiddled around in my room for a little bit, packing some stuff away. I mucked around with the sleeping bag for a while, but my room was too small to even pack my stuff. I became frustrated and went down for breakfast. It was a little after 7am and I was still the first to arrive. I ordered egg chapatti and a pot of milk tea and sat down to watch the snow falling outside. A thermometer in the dining hall that had been set up to take a remote reading from outside read -19 degrees. *Brrrrrr*. The yak dung fire was already in full swing, and once inside I had to layer down a few.

I'm not too sure how you mess up chapatti; a round, whole wheat flour-based bread of Indian origin with egg on top, but they did. It wasn't a loss of appetite from altitude either, I was ravenous. The bread was way too floury and hadn't set properly in the middle. It tasted like it was cooked on the yak dung fire. No pan on top – just straight over the fire. I tried, but I couldn't eat it. It tasted like smoky yak crap. I filled myself instead on the 1.5 litres of milky tea enforced with way too much sugar.

Subash had woken, seen the weather and gone back to sleep, so he didn't surface until after I'd 'finished' my breakfast. I went back upstairs and just sat on my bed and tried to catch my breath. I had no intention of packing, I was going to wait until Nima knocked on my door and then I was going to get him to do it for me. I'm not ashamed of it either. He was just over half my size and would find it far easier to pack a bag in a shoe box than I would. Instead I grabbed my boots and sat on them in a vain attempt to thaw them out. I'm from the tropics. I don't know how to unfreeze boots without a microwave.

Nima came and packed for me while I kind of fiddled around with my camera. When he was finished I kind of almost had enough room to put my boots on. Then we were off! It was back the way we had come. We climbed steeply out of Gorak Shep just as the last few flurries of snow settled on the ground. I stopped and looked back. Kallar Pathar was still cloaked in cloud, but perhaps the top 500 metres of Pumori had burst through and stood proudly in the morning sunshine. It was quite a sight to behold. We carried on and passed trekkers in dribs and drabs coming the opposite way. They were slow and weary looking and I didn't envy them in the slightest. We were, in contrast, positively skipping off the mountain. It was for the most part downhill and we were absolutely flying. Every metre of elevation we lost I found a new lease on life.

We came to the top of the rise on which I had overtaken the Koreans and stood and stared in amazement as a hoard of trekkers scampered up the valley in the opposite direction. This was the real Khumbu Highway. There were hundreds of them. A large group had already collapsed on rocks at the top and were busy attempting to get air and water in their bodies, while an ant-like trekker trail was carving its way up the hill as many more joined at the bottom. And then looking out there were people coming from everywhere. If I'd been a day later I would have had an even more miserable time in Gorak Shep. Subash and I stared at each other in wonder.

'Wow you is a very luckys man,' he said.

'I think so.'

'With all these people impossible to find room for one persons. If you stay in Gorak Shep tonight you is sleeping in the restaurant!'

'Next to the mixed fried noodles?'

'Maybe,' he said with a smile on his face.

We began making our way quickly down the slope. As with the day before, people ascending stopped and stared with wonder and mild exasperation at our ability to move with such haste. Just the day before I had thought it superhuman, and now I was that man.

'You gotta love it, don't cha?' an overweight but exceedingly friendly American man rhetorically asked me as I went past him.

'Absolutely!' I replied. 'Hey, this hill is the hardest thing you'll do today. It's pretty steady after that.'

'Right on, buddy,' he answered and he slapped me on the back as a huge smile encompassed his whole face. I could have been friends with that man, but alas we had many miles to go. I turned on my heel and recommenced the descent, drawing praise and wonder from everyone as we went. The next day, hundreds of people headed back down the mountain with a spring in their step, thinking that the big, hairy bloke wearing the t-shirt wasn't that supernatural after all.

'Holy shit, I think I see the firefighters,' I said to Subash. I could tell because Rob wore bloody ridiculous, light-blue leg protectors all the way up to his knees, which he was currently sporting with a pair of shorts.

'Yes, is them!' Subash confirmed.

I had a quick chat with them. Steve had a serious case of mountain sickness and therefore they both had to turn their back on the Renjo La. He told me he thought his head was going to explode. He had a hideous-looking lump the size of a golf ball on his neck, and all-in-all the two of them looked like shit. I gave them my best, keen to get the hell away before I was subjected to a story involving ladders, fire extinguishers and grannies trapped in chairs.

It wasn't long before Lobuche came into view. Subash hawked and spat on the ground. *Quite right.* He enquired if I needed a rest, but on finding out it was only one hour to the next town, I opted to carry on. I'd seen enough of Lobuche in this life-time. We followed the same path for some 15 minutes, before it branched off from the turn-off to Cho La. I looked down at the vast snowfield that we had plodded across two days before, and was slightly mortified to see two huge gaping puddles right where the path had been. One was about half the size of a football field.

'Umm Subash,' I said in my most nonchalant of voices. 'You know that giant

235

snowfield we crossed two days ago? That wasn't a snowfield was it? That was a lake, right?'

'That one there?' he asked. 'Yes is lake.'

'But we walked straight over the middle of it.'

'Yes it was a frozens.'

'Yes, but now it's not.'

'No problems man, frozen two days ago.'

'But how did you know how thick the ice was?'

'Because I am the guides!'

I left it at that.

I looked to the west one final time and traced our route back up the valley to the Cho La Pass, shuddered slightly, then stepped onto yet another new path. We came across a large yak train on a rather narrow path covered in deep snow. We actually had to step off the trail and dig ourselves a new snow ledge and we had to do it quick. Yaks wait for no man. I looked ahead to see Nima high up away from the track, forging a new way effortlessly through knee-deep snow. It was very impressive. The path began to curve around to the east so quickly that we couldn't see more than 20-or-so metres in front of us, the mountain wall obscuring the rest of it from view.

When it eventually straightened up, greeting us was a great deal of stone cairns scattered around randomly on the ensuing flat ground. Prayer flags joined a few of them together. These were the memorials to all the people that lost their lives climbing Mt Everest. Saw-tooth peaks cut the sky in a mesmerising 360-degree panorama, lending a most climactic feeling to these people's lives, as though they were *meant* to end up here. A more dramatic and fitting location there never was. I sought out a pile of stones larger than most. Wind-blown snow had covered the last three letters of his name, but I knew it already. It was the memorial to Scott Fischer, the climbing guide that had perished in the infamous 1996 climbing disaster on Everest, immortally recorded in Jon Krakauer's excellent book *Into Thin Air*.

We stayed for perhaps 10 minutes, sitting in silent contemplation in this most sombre of places. Then we got up and walked across yet another pass, this time the Thok La at 4830m, before dropping down just over 200 vertical metres to a place called Dughla in a little under 20 minutes. It was straight down. We passed a few trekkers coming the other way, all of whom looked absolutely spent, but still had a way to go before getting to Lobuche.

Dughla was almost completely wiped out in 2007 by what they call a glacial lake outburst flood (GLOF) and now it comprises only a couple of buildings perched kind of haphazardly out in the open on the middle of a fairly relentless slope. It just seemed a bizarre place to put a settlement. We stopped and I topped up with water while sitting outside in a large courtyard. The place was teeming with trekkers, most of whom had stopped for lunch en route to Lobuche. I can imagine them getting there, looking up at the climb ahead and thinking they'd rather get some noodles and tea in them before attempting such a thing.

We weren't there for long, having decided to push on to Pheriche for lunch. The sun was shining in Dughla yet as soon as we stepped onto the path it disappeared and was replaced by an ugly, black cloud that was dumping a serious amount of snow on us. The path was narrow at first and we had to pause and step uphill to allow the throngs of trekking groups to guide themselves around us. Some were friendly and some were not. In one group, I think they were kiwis, every single person thanked me for stepping aside. It was quite funny. It went like this:

'Thank you!'

'You're welcome.'

'Thanks.'

'Not a problem.'

'Thank you.'

'It's ok.'

'Ta.'

'You bet.'

'Thanks.'

'No worries.'

'Thank you!'

'Ok.'

I just smiled at the last seven people. I'd had enough. The track widened out and before long we had entered a full-blown valley. It was a weird valley. Most are either v-shaped (formed by water) or u-shaped glaciated valleys, but this was a mixture of the two, alternating as the miles carried it further and further away from my sight. I'd have to say that it was an old v-shaped valley that had its interlocking spurs only partially carved out by a later glacier, but that it was a very long time ago so that erosion has begun to mask the actual shape of the glaciated valley.

We could see Pheriche, far away at the end of the valley, but before long the clouds rolled in, dumping more snow and shielding the town from our view. We wandered through little channels, perhaps about knee-depth, I guess formed by heavy monsoonal rain or even by the floodwater from seven years ago. There was certainly only evidence of a small stream flowing gently through this valley now. The channels were complex and gave us many different paths to choose from, but invariably all headed roughly in the right direction. At times streams in varying widths flowed off the valley walls and these we forded by way of stepping stones that I presume had been placed there for our benefit, although they almost looked like they existed there naturally.

I stumbled upon Pheriche rather unexpectedly at first. I had been so consumed with where I was putting my feet that I realised I hadn't looked up in ages. We were at the end of the valley and I found myself having to negotiate some oncoming traffic in the form of widely spread out yaks. They were normally in Indian file, so this was uncharted waters for me. I had just been thinking about what on earth I was going to call this story. Nothing obvious had really jumped out at me. I was just thinking, *wouldn't it be good if I got chased by a yak for about two feet, then I could call the story Yak Attack, or Attack of the Yak.* Then I looked up and saw the size of these hairy beasts and retracted my mental statement immediately.

'I could call it *No Yak Attack,*' I muttered to the first yak that came my way, then I began dodging them with the agility of a new-born giraffe. I emerged out the other side unscathed, but still without a title.

'This place is alright!' I said enthusiastically to Subash and Nima while I was theatrically turning my head around. It wasn't huge – a dozen lodges were dotted along a very wide main 'road' – but it certainly was agreeable. Maybe everything was agreeable compared with Lobuche. We ducked into one of the lodge/restaurants for a spot of lunch.

'Oh my God they have rosti!' I shouted. I was way too excited over potatoes for a man my age. On the wall stood a poster advertising something called Sea Buckthorn Juice. It was made from the sea buckthorn berry and was grown right here in the Khumbu region. It was meant to contain more vitamin C than oranges, and it said that I'd be supporting the local farmers if I ordered some. Down the wall a bit was a picture of the Dalai Lama, who appeared to be sitting in this very room. He must have paid a visit.

'I'll have rosti with two fried eggs, a cup of milk tea and a sea buckthorn juice please Subash,' I said, and he went off and placed my order. We were in a large, rectangular wooden building with ginormous windows that stretched from the chairs, which lined the perimeter of the room, to the ceiling. As we sat there the clouds lifted and dissipated slightly and a stream of daylight came pouring into the valley. The temperature of the room went from a little above freezing to way above it and I had to remove my jacket.

A very small, middle-aged lady came out moments later with my drinks, but to my disappointment the juice had been heated up. It was so hard to get a cold drink in this country. The first sip of this bright orange tonic was tongue-shrivelling-ly sour, yet I went back for more. After becoming accustomed to the taste, which really was by the time I was at the bottom of the glass, it had actually become quite agreeable. So I ordered one more. It was the first vitamin C I'd had in days that hadn't come in tablet form so I lapped it up. The rosti was just OK. Yet, it was wonderfully filling, which is of course why I ordered it in the first place. We still had a couple of hours to make our way to Pangboche, where we'd be laying our weary heads that night, so sustenance was required. I was also really getting sick of Snickers bars. I'm sad to say it but it's true. I will have to have another go at sea level to make sure it isn't just the altitude playing tricks with my mind.

I paid the bill and we got up and walked out, just as a monster cloud engulfed the sun and began trying to systematically bury us in snow. *That'd be right,* I thought, as I was instantly forced back inside my jacket and beanie. Looking back at where we had come from it was getting dark. It looked like Lobuche was about to get smacked by a real snowstorm. We'd gotten down at precisely the right time. Everything had been timed well really. Imagine being up there in that miserable weather with all those people? That would be a real nightmare. I shuddered, or maybe shivered, then put my feet into gear.

The valley abruptly turned on a dog-leg to the south-west, or to our right as we were looking at it, and we were forced to climb out of Pheriche over the Pheriche pass before plunging down the other side to join the roaring Imja Khola River. Had we wanted to, we could have turned 180 degrees and followed this river all the way to its source, taking us to Chhukhung and Island Peak Base Camp. But that wasn't our path. We were going back to civilisation. Well, Kathmandu. If that counts?

'Why did we just have to go all the way over that pass to come back down here to the same level?' I asked Subash.

'This is the paths, man,' he answered.

'Yes but it was so unnecessary.'

He stopped walking and turned around to face me. He had a strange look on his face. It could have been disappointment.

'Look, all I'm saying is that you go over a pass if you have no possible alternative. I would have built that path following that lovely river down there on flat ground. But you Nepalese see a hill and think: "I'm going to build a path right over the highest point of that," whereas in Australia we avoid tricky feats of engineering at all costs. If we were putting a road here, I guarantee you we wouldn't be going all the way up there.'

He shrugged, smiled, and kept on walking. He knew I was ranting now. Wasting breaths. Wasting time. I saw a big hill as time to climb. Subash saw flat ground. He went up that slope like it was flat ground. If you really prompted him further on the subject, he might cave in

244

and say it was 'a gradual up', but then he'd most certainly say it was flat because we went down the other side, thus rendering the climb invalid. Tis the Nepali logic.

We could see Pangboche now. It was about five kilometres straight down the valley. We couldn't see her, but we were standing right at the base of Ama Dablam. Every now and then I'd look up and try to pierce the clouds with my vision, but to no avail. This was the closest I'd ever be to the mountain that had first inspired me to come to this region, and I couldn't even see it. We had been incredibly lucky with the weather, so I was still content. You can't have it all. The going was easy too. A little up, but mostly we headed down. The snow followed us all the way to Pangboche and in fact became thicker the more we descended. At some point we dropped below the 4000m mark for the last time. It felt wonderful.

We strolled through a couple of small villages, paused to make stupid noises at some new-born puppies that could barely open their eyes, and before long we were in Pangboche. It was a decent-sized place, but every building was a lodge. We wandered most of the way through town before coming to the Eco-Holiday Lodge, a quaint-looking two-story building. There were bricks for the ground floor and white timber boards for the top, capped with a green corrugated iron roof. It had a large grass courtyard out the front that was intersected by a raised, stone path that headed for the entrance. However, there was a half-yak, half-cow standing on this path staring at us, blocking the way. *Half a Yak Attack* – I thought, here we go; but Subash turned cattle herder once more and shooed the dopey creature away.

'Later this whole yard will be a full of the yaks,' he said.

My room had three single beds pushed together, which made it look king-sized. I was startled to realise that today we'd come all the way from Gorak Shep with that two-thirds-of-a-single-sized bed, and all of a sudden that felt like a very long time ago. I was delighted. Nima strolled into the room a few minutes later. I thanked him and told him to go to the dining room while I changed my shoes.

I was a little bit excited, you see, because I had been taken off the booze ban. We were now at 3900 metres and going down, so alcohol was back on the menu. I bought the boys many drinks as thanks for their hard work. We started with Everest Beer, but it wasn't long before we got stuck in to the local Kukri Rum. So we passed a snowy night, huddled around a yak shit fire, drinking cheap, cheap rum from the bottle, and telling stories from home. We were all away from home, after all. The yard filled with yaks, as promised. They were all different shapes, colours and sizes, much like humans I supposed. They seemed to just walk down the lane through Pangboche and then turn into the yard all by themselves. They were completely unsupervised, but they just knew what to do. Definitely not like humans.

*

I awoke with daylight streaming in through the curtains, which weren't large enough for the window frame. I remembered the night before, trying to find some equilibrium in the final curtain resting place, but in the end decided that a large gap down the middle was better than two gaps on either side. It seems trivial now. I'd drank a litre of water overnight, and that, combined with lower altitude, fresh mountain air, a comfortable bed and a good night's sleep saw me emerge into the dining room fit and ready to go.

I dined and paid the bill. I was gobsmacked. One night's accommodation, dinner, breakfast and a tonne of drinks came to about $40. I felt like I was ripping them off. Then I felt even worse, knowing that Nima and Subash could not afford to drink beer and rum at these places, despite the costs seeming so low to us foreigners. What to do?

We wandered out into the crisp, fresh air and looked back from whence we had come. There was Ama Dablam. We had walked right past it. It was windy at 6800 metres. Ama Dablam was doing an Everest impression, having snow wind-blasted from its summit. Right next to us, and just as spectacular, Kangtega rose above to dizzying heights.

Before long Tengboche came into view, perched up on a little pass in a clearing, but surrounded by a snow-cloaked pine forest. We spent the morning heading downwards before crossing Imja Khola and heading back up on the far side of the bank. This area was sheltered from the sun and was quite icy. We climbed for about two minutes, but were forced over to the cliff face by the largest procession of yaks I'd seen in three whole weeks. They weren't together, but each herder probably had between five and eight yaks under his control, but all-in-all there would have been close to 200 of them plodding down the hill. There was nothing for it; we had to wait.

We climbed a little rise to get off the path, and stood there in knee-deep snow and waited. It began to get really cold. Well, it already was cold, it's just that I'd stopped so I really began to feel it. We were there for probably half an hour before we could get going again. The only difficulty now was that the snow on the ground had been compacted by a hundred tonne of yak, and it was now extremely icy and difficult to walk on. We laboured up the slope slowly, slipping occasionally. Nima had had enough, so he once again broke a new-yet-precarious-looking trail a little higher up on a steep slope. Only he could do that. Well only a Sherpa anyway. Even Subash did not care for it. We came to a little section where the path headed back down. It was only 30 metres long, but it looked like a bob sled track. Subash turned and said, 'There is only one way to do this.'

He turned and faced the ice. Then he did something entirely unexpected. He assumed a really, really girly running technique and took off down the slope with arms flailing everywhere. It bloody worked too! He didn't fall once.

'See how I did it?' he called. 'Your turn.'

I looked around for a lucky egg to kiss, but didn't find one; then remembered that Sanka always crashed anyway, even with the lucky egg. I took off and started flapping my arms. It really worked! Every time I began to lose control of my foot, this would be offset by a flapping arm and I would regain my composure. Before I knew it I was down.

'Now you know how to get down icy slope,' he said.

'Yeah, it's fine, as long as no one is watching.'

'Watching no problems.'

'Ok.'

And we were off like a bride's nighty, charging up the slope to Tengboche. It was so easy. I barely had to breathe at this altitude to get enough oxygen. My lungs were chock-full of red blood cells and they had the easiest job in the world at the moment. A pack of yaks (or whatever a group of yaks are called) began to catch us as we climbed. *Ahhh a challenge!* We quickened our pace and climbed into the sunshine through the heavily scented pine forest. The extra warm air began to melt the snow, and before long a little trickle of water began to flow between the stones that formed our path. We climbed twenty minutes into ever-rising temperatures before wading through some deep mud infused with yak poo poo. The gradient was easing off and before I realised it we were strolling casually into Tengboche.

That kept happening to me. At the beginning of the trip I'd gasp my way into a town, always looking around the next bend and hoping for civilisation. Now I was stumbling on them by accident. They were almost coming up too soon. I looked down at my boots and with more than just a touch of pride, I can announce that there was about one millimetre of mud lining the side of my soles and my pants were yak-crap free. I beamed. I wish those locals from all those days ago could see me now.

Tengboche was an agreeable sort of place. We came across the monastery and sat down on the stairs to recover. A monk was out the front sweeping dirt off the stairs. I had really wanted to see this monastery, but it was closed in the morning for meditation and reflection and we had arrived too early. Instead we gazed back the way we had come. Ama Dablam was beginning to attract a bit of attention in the form of some persistent morning clouds that, discounting the day before, we had yet to see. We were really so lucky with the weather. Anyone arriving in the mountains this morning would have been left bitterly disappointed, as Mount Everest was already disappearing into a swirl of grey and white. I sat there and watched it for a while, the largest mountain in the world; but in a matter of moments it was gone from view again. She liked to hide, old Chomolungma.

'Will I see Everest again?' I asked.

'Of course,' said Subash. 'You see it from Phakding to Namche so maybe you also is seeing it from the Namche to Phakding, no?'

'Ah yes, of course.'

Of course it didn't matter. I had been circling Everest for weeks like a hunter circles its prey. I had seen it from more angles than most people have the privilege of doing. I was a very lucky man.

There was no point in hanging around in Tengboche. It was a lovely little place, and under different circumstances I could have stayed there and relaxed for a little while. It had the spirituality, the mountain views and a bakery. What more could you want?

It was more or less straight down for 400 vertical metres to the next village, Phunke Tenga, which essentially sits at the confluence between the Imja Khola and Dudh Khosi rivers at 3250m above sea level. It was steep going down so I felt sorry for the poor buggers puffing and panting their way up in the opposite direction. Even most of the porters I passed were sitting on their little 'T' sticks enjoying a well-earned rest. Of course it didn't take long to drop the altitude and we cruised into a warm Phunke a little after 11am. It was too early for lunch and we were still two hours from Namche Bazaar, so Subash was trying to force feed me some tucker. I wasn't hungry, but I appeased him when I ordered some dried noodles in a packet to munch on. The rest of the morning we'd spend regaining a lot of that lost altitude.

'I'm sorry man but we must going ups,' said Subash as I was chomping on the noodles.

'No problem man, not many of the ups left,' I said. 'I am going to try and enjoy it.'

You know what? I did enjoy it. I was fit and healthy and on holiday. I liked what a guide book on the region had said. Just paraphrasing here, but it said something like, try *not to think of it as walking to your destination, but more that you have already arrived, and now you're just on a nice pleasant stroll enjoying some of the greatest scenery on earth.* I like that a lot.

We went up past little tacky villages selling tacky touristy crap before going past the township of Khumjung. Here the path widened out enough to accommodate a car, but of course it had no way of getting there. An old man sat on a stool by the side of the path with a donation box and ledger. Subash told me they took donations to build this path, and they would continue to take them to improve other paths in the area. He told me that a few years ago this fantastic road we now wandered was in an awful state and they desperately needed foreign investment to improve it.

I thought of some of the walking tracks I'd stumbled over and how dangerous some of them were, and so I gave a small donation to the man. He'd not said a word when we had approached him, or as I donated the money, yet as soon as the rupee note hit the bottom of the box he became animated and thanked me very much while calling out: 'Namaste! Namaste! Darnaybaad!' I almost jumped off the path.

'Thank you man,' said Subash as we were leaving.

'My pleasure.'

We carried on the wide road all the way to Namche Bazaar, passing a good many Buddhist Stupas and prayer flags as we went. I was beginning to get tired and hungry. The first houses of Namche Bazaar appeared at about 2pm and I was so unbelievably happy to be entering the top of the town this time. On the way up you get to town, but still have to climb up for 15 minutes to get to your destination, which doesn't sound like a lot unless you are the one doing the climbing. The Sherpa Village Guesthouse awaited me, as did a big, delicious plate of rosti with two fried eggs.

Chapter Eighteen

LUKLA

Nima, Subash and myself hit the beer. Then we smashed the rum. There was no responsible service of alcohol at this bar. Back home alcohol is measured out in units or shots, but here the jigga was the size of a mug of tea, and the lady filled it right to the brim. Sometimes she didn't consider this to be enough and so she added another splash for good measure. It wasn't long before Nima was absolutely hammered. It happened so quick that it was entirely unexpected. He stumbled around the lounge room, tried to hold conversations with me in Nepali, but when he realised I was, in fact, his client, he reverted to his pigeon English to tell me the same story for about the sixteenth time. It was all very sloppy. At 7pm he was essentially kicked out of the dining room by a combination of Subash and the management and it took him 25 minutes to say goodnight, which included a 10-minute hand shake. Finally he left.

'Wow that was interesting!' I said to Subash.

'The Nima is the very drunk.'

'Oh no he's back!'

Nima fell through the door, picked himself up and said, 'Good night, sir, I going the sleep place now, sir.'

'I don't know that you are, but good night!'

'Yes sir. One time Japanese expedition chun fi trip shwaga da.'

'Ah yes, that's the Japanese story you have already told me seven times.'

Subash grabbed Nima gently by his shirt and said something to him in Nepali.

'Good night, sir!' Nima shouted, causing everyone in the packed room to turn around and stare at us, before he left the room once more.

'You know he is going to the porter's houses and he will be drinking more stuffs for sure,' Subash told me.

'More? He is absolutely hammered, he shouldn't be drinking more.'

'The Nima is a man. The Nima can do whatever he is liking to do.'

Nima walked outside and he went the wrong way, so it wasn't long before I saw him stumble back in the opposite direction. My eyes drifted to the door. It opened and then shut again without him coming back in. I think maybe the cold air had sobered him up ever so slightly and he'd come to his senses.

I ordered the Yak steak, I had to try it. It came out in the tiniest of pieces and was drowned in gravy. It was a little chewy, but I quite liked it.

*

The morning weather had returned to its former glory and the stroll down the mountain was most pleasant. I ignored the pain that was shooting through my knee with every downward step, knowing full well that most people had sore knees on this stage of the trek. I could only hope that it wasn't going to give up on me now, having come so far and being so close to the finish line. Depending on my knee, this could be the last day of trekking for us. If I was in too much pain we'd halt once more in Phakding, if not we were aiming to get to Lukla, the place with the scary airstrip carved into the side of a mountain that we were due to fly out of in two days. But flights were forever being cancelled and rescheduled as the whole operation was weather permitting.

It was advisable to get to Lukla as early as humanly possible to reconfirm flights and jump on them if the weather was clear. We heard many horror stories about people being stuck in Lukla in a cloud for over a week, which caused them to miss their international flights back home from Kathmandu. It worked the other way too, with people being stuck in Kathmandu for days on end before they are able to fly to Lukla to begin their treks. I thought Namche Bazaar had been very quiet while I was there, because on the way up the mountain the place was humming. It turns out that flights had been interrupted from Kathmandu, and some people were now three days behind schedule. *Should have walked in from Jiri*, I thought from my high horse.

The Everest viewpoint was choc-a-bloc with people and for good reason. The skies were cloud-free and the air was crystal clear, and Everest sat there looking rather proud and important. It didn't look that far away in the radiant sunshine. I said my good byes, snapped a picture over the shoulder of a middle-aged man and then continued going down. We meandered our way down the slope, but occasionally we made our own, much steeper path directly down, the shortest distance between two points being a straight line. We were heading back the same way that we had come, so we did the necessary crossings of the Dudh Khosi a good five or six times before wandering into Phakding at about lunchtime.

I dined once more in the Beer Garden Lodge, delighted that I was the only one in there (no goddam restaurant yoga practising hippy types with smug, Australian middle-aged women). I ate my delicious bowl of spaghetti, washed it down with an even nicer cup of masala tea, stood up and did a few practise hops on my bad knee, and deciding that it wasn't too bad I paid my bill, summoned Subash and hit the trail for the final time. I was a little bit sad and solemn until the track started heading back up a steep slope. It reminded me of 25 days of pain and weariness and all of a sudden I was delighted. A faster changing of the tune had never before happened.

'Man I am feeling the bads,' said Subash randomly and breaking a long period of silence.

'Why man, what's wrong?'

'I speaks to the chef yesterday, he my friend, and he is saying this was not the Yaks.'

'You mean what I had for dinner?'

'Yes man, it was not the Yaks.'

'Oh God, what the hell was it then?' I asked, alarm beginning to enter my voice. All I could think was *dog, dog, dog, dog!*

'I am so sorry man. It was the buffalo.'

I breathed a huge sigh of relief.

'Not dog then?'

'No not the dog!' He shouted while bursting into a fit of laughter. 'We don't eat the dogs, man.'

'Oh thank God! That's not so bad. I've eaten buffalo before many times back home. It's pretty bad though, advertising they have yak steak and then giving you something else. They should have said, 'Sorry, we don't have any yak, would you like buffalo instead?' That is seriously illegal in Australia.'

'Yes man but the yaks is very rare and expensive. They never is having the yaks. The yaks is worth more money alive.'

'Doesn't make it right, Subash. They are lying to people. But thank you for telling me, I appreciate your honesty.'

We passed the turn-off for Jiri and kept going straight after Subash had enquired if I was certain I wanted to fly out. I had never been more certain about anything in my life. We continued going up until the final pass came into view, emphasised by a walk-through archway and a cluster of prayer flags flapping carelessly in the surrounding trees. We gained the top as a group of school children laughed and carried on in the archway. We were in bloody Lukla.

'You didn't tell me the town was right here!' I cried, a little bit peeved that I couldn't enjoy the last few steps of the trek. They were already taken.

'Another surprise,' Subash said smiling, and I joined in. It did actually feel really good to be here. Lukla felt a bit like Times Square after where I'd been. There were people everywhere, and all of them were talking on mobile phones. It was quite surreal. We made our way most of the way through town to our lodge for the night. I was promised a hot shower in my room, but the hot water system was broken. What was one more night? I could wait until Kathmandu.

It was incredibly novel to have a western toilet in my room. I hadn't had that kind of luxury for close to four weeks and now I wouldn't have to go through that whole getting-dressed-in-the-middle-of-the-night charade in order to go to the dunny. The bathroom itself had a huge window and no curtain, which afforded excellent views of Lukla while sitting on the throne, but didn't offer anything in the way of privacy. To combat that I just sat as still as a statue and pretended I wasn't using the toilet. I'm not sure how effective it was, but it was all I had.

We sat in the smokiest of dinner lounges and drank some Kukri Rum, poured in even larger measuring jiggas than in Namche Bazaar and eavesdropped on some of the conversations fellow trekkers were having around us. Most of them were 'on their way up', heading into the High Himalaya having flown into Lukla sometime that day. Everyone was drinking and everyone was excited. *I wonder how excited they'll feel when they have to tackle the Himalayan-sized ascents with a hangover,* I contemplated, but didn't feel the need to pass on that insight. I wasn't going to be *that* wet blanket. Besides, I was drinking a quarter bottle of rum in every cup, so who was I to pass judgement?

People began to disappear early from the hall. Perhaps they weren't that silly. I took my leave of Subash and went up to my room. It was only 8pm, but I was stuffed. It had been a big day. It had been a big three-and-a-half weeks. I walked into my room and switched on the toilet light, which did a supernova impression and ended up being easily the brightest thing in Lukla. It made heads turn as far away as Europe. I imagined using the toilet lit up like a Christmas tree for all to see, flicked the lights back off, but kept the door to my room slightly ajar to allow a controlled amount of light to creep in. I knew everyone could see me, but what the hell? I was flying out in the morning and I'd never see these people again.

*

I awoke just as the sun began to change the sky from black to dark blue, meaning that it was early, but not that early.

'Mmmmm, 5.45!' I guessed out loud. It was 5.52am and I was getting good at this. I'd had more than enough sleep, but we were still in the mountains and it was still cold, so I pulled the covers tight and smiled. *You don't have to walk anywhere today you lucky so and so!* I did that thing where you squirm around the bed, but it doesn't matter what position you end up in because every position is divinely comfortable. I laid there, recounting every single day of the trek and I was filled with a sense of wonder. *Holy shit, I'm in Lukla!* And that meant one thing. One thing that I had been dreading for perhaps the last five years: the flight out of Lukla Airport's airstrip.

I ordered the rosti with two fried eggs, but it only came with one. I was disappointed, but not to the point of whingeing, realising that I was likely to sit on my arse for the rest of the day (if I didn't drop off the face of a mountain), and that two fried eggs were probably a little bit extravagant for a non-trekker. Subash told me that it hadn't been possible to get Nima on the same flight as us. The price we pay for a Nepali to fly with us is considerably less than the cost of the ticket we buy as tourists (I'm not exactly sure, but I think their ticket was less than half the cost) so obviously the airlines try to fit as many foreigners on their planes as possible. Lowly porters are last in line, I'm afraid, and there was no ticket for Nima that day.

I now knew that I only had about 10 minutes with Nima left, which made me quite sad. I thought of all the times I'd seen my Sherpa friend carving his way, knee deep, through virgin snow while a perfectly good path loomed just inches from him. He loved it. Nay, it was in his blood and it was all he knew, and he was more at home in the mountains than anyone else I'd seen in my days in the Himalaya.

I knew the amount of money that Nima was paid by the agency to carry my backpack around all day, and while it's not my place to divulge such information, I'm sure you can guess that it is not a lot of money. Both the guides and the porters rely on tips from their clients to beef up their salaries, and I felt bad that they sometimes take out backpackers that had spent all their money already on the trip, with nothing left over to reward the people that had shared these memories with them. I am a very fortunate person in this world, in that I can afford to travel to other countries to see places and see how people live their lives, and I was deeply moved by the simplicity in which my friends Subash and Nima lived theirs.

'Nima, I want to thank you for everything that you have done for me,' I said, deliberately slowly, so that he would absorb every word I'd said to him. 'Without you, I would not have made it over the passes.'

'No problem, sir,' he said, although there was sincerity in his voice.

'I want you to have this,' I continued, handing him an envelope that he quickly tucked into his jacket, out of sight.

'Thank you, sir,' he said while looking up uncharacteristically into my eyes. I put my hand out to shake his, as we do in our culture. He grabbed it and shook it for a few seconds before moving my hand up in between his into a praying motion. He then moved all three hands up until they stopped just below his chin, which he then met with a slight, but controlled bow of the head.

I choked back a lump that had formed in my throat, nodded my head, picked up my day pack and said, 'Take me to the airport!''

'Ok, sir!' Nima kicked back into porter mode, dived into the straps of my bag for one last time, and was off like a porter with a pack.

'Even the bloody way to Lukla airstrip is uphill!' I complained in good spirits one last time.

'This is the mountain,' replied Subash, who turned around and burst into laughter when he saw that I was joking. 'This is looking a very flat me.'

I relished every cobbled step that I climbed, positively hopping and skipping from one to another. I bet I looked a right knob-head. Sorry, just finished watching Billy Elliot. But I'm sure I looked pretty silly. I saw a gigantic airfield sock flapping in the breeze, and we walked around the perimeter of a barbed-wire fence before looking down on Lukla runway where I stood dead in my tracks and just stared. The horrifying steepness of it was only superseded by its length, which seemed to drop off a cliff within spitting distance.

First things first. I'm not a wuss and I'm definitely not an adrenalin junky, but somehow I have found a happy equilibrium in my life. I have bungy jumped once, which was utterly terrifying at the time, but immediately after it was finished I wanted to do it again (although I was happy at the same time that it was too expensive to do again). I love roller coasters, but I'm still undecided as to whether or not I'd throw myself out of a plane.

According to an article in Britain's *Daily Mail* in March, 2013 that followed the Sita Air Flight 601 crash of September the previous year:

'The old dirt strip was tarmacked in 1999, but landing at Lukla is still a challenge. Just 1,500ft long and only 60ft wide, the runway

ends in a blank mountain wall and has an uphill gradient of 12 per cent.

Only STOL (short take-off and landing) aircraft, like the Dornier 228 or Twin Otter, are able to land in such a short distance. Overshoot and you crash into the hillside at its end. Undershoot and you plough into the steep hillside beneath.

Both have happened. The approach can only be attempted in good weather as there are still no navigational aids.'

Something had red-flagged this moment in my brain as something I should be worried about. A plane has crashed while attempting to land at Lukla seven times in the past seven years (even discounting the Sita Air flight that was bound for Lukla, but had to turn back minutes after take-off after apparently flying into a vulture. They crashed on the way back to Kathmandu, killing all 19 people on board, including seven Brits, five Chinese and seven Nepalese). There hasn't been a crash involving a plane since 2010, although in September 2013 a helicopter crashed after its tail came in contact with the barbed-wire fence surrounding the perimeter. So I guess Lukla was due for another one.

Granted, there had been tens of thousands of flights take off and land in Lukla since the last crash, but somehow it was just the fact that we'd be dropping off the side of the mountain that got to me. One week away from my departure in February, 2014 to Kathmandu, I jumped on the internet and did what you do from time to time, you Google things. On this particular occasion I Googled Nepal, hit enter, and was deeply disturbed to read about eight articles with the sub label 'two hours ago' about that horrible crash involving a Nepal Airlines flight from Pokhara that disappeared into the mountains, claiming the lives of all 18 people. Nepal's air-safety record is absolutely woeful, to say the least.

There is such a thing as the 'EU Air Safety List', which details lists of banned airlines by country from landing in any European airport. They list 18 banned airlines for Nepal, or all of them.

Fast forward to 2016, I typed 'Nepal' into Google's search once again, and this was the article, once again updated 'two hours ago' on *CNN.com*:

Two days after fatal crash, another plane goes down in Nepal, killing two

'A plane crashed in the mountains of northwest Nepal on Friday, killing the two pilots and injuring nine passengers, authorities said. This was Nepal's second aviation tragedy in just three days.

The Air Kasthamandap flight involved in Friday's crash was carrying 11 people. The single-engine plane was heading from Nepalgunj in the country's southwest to the Jumla district in the northwest, said Bhola Guragain, director of the Tribhuvan Airport Operations Department.

Witnesses told the Kathmandu Post that the plane descended steeply and crashed nose-down.

The plane crashed in a field in the mountains in the Kalikot district, said Binod G.C., a police officer in the district.

The latest accident occurred just two days after a Tara Air plane crashed midway through a 19-minute flight, killing all 23 people aboard.

Poor weather and dense fog are believed to be the causes of Wednesday's crash. The bodies of all the victims have been recovered.

Both planes crashed in northern, mountainous parts of Nepal, but the crash sites *are more than 100 miles (160 kilometres) apart.'*

Flying in Nepal is not safe. And it is not getting any safer.

But back in the present, Subash was calling to me after a short eternity in la-la land: 'We can still walk to the Jiri if you is wanting this.'

'Never again!' I cried, using hyperbole to great effect.

A security guard stood at the entrance to the airport, barking orders at people and really just making a nuisance of himself. Subash began a heated debate with the man, who would not be swayed no matter how hard my guide worked his rhetoric.

'The Nima is not allowed inside,' said Subash. 'You is needing the boarding pass to get inside.'

'We don't have boarding passes yet,' I said.

Subash frowned at me, his impatience growing. *Why do you have to be so trivial?* he said to me with his eyes.

'Ok Nima, thank you again for everything my friend,' I said, putting my hand on the small

272

man's shoulder. He grinned the widest of grins. 'No wait!' I almost shouted. 'We don't have a photo of the three of us. Now who could possibly take it, Subash?' I added, except this time I motioned furiously to the security guard with my head, indicating that Subash should request a photo.

'Ok I will ask him,' he replied, although he was highly reluctant to ask the guard for some reason. He asked and the guard burst into the greatest smile that up until that moment, I hadn't thought possible from such a rude person. I guessed he was one of those stuck-being-a-soldier-for-a-living-because-photography-doesn't-put-bread-on-the-table-in-Nepal kind of people, hence why he was so nasty. I forgave him immediately and gave him a quick rundown of the camera.

Well, I know he had three fantastic models, which aided the process greatly, but the man actually took a really good photo. He was delighted when I told him to take another one just in case (meanwhile porters everywhere had seized the opportunity to carry in their client's bags to the terminal building behind this man's back. It was like a terrible spy spoof, like *Austin Powers* or something equally as awful, whereby we had engaged the security guard in an entirely implausible distraction).

I turned and shook Nima's hand one last time. He flashed me that brilliant, genuine smile and we said our goodbyes. I turned to walk into the terminal building with my large backpack back under my charge. We walked into a zoo without rules. People pushed in front of other people and others spat on the tiled ground while everyone was shouting and carrying on as though this were the final day of Earth. Subash was worth his weight in gold that morning. He grabbed my backpack off me and kind of used it as a battering ram to knock unsuspecting souls out of his way. He became a human cannon ball and only the very foolish stood in his path. He found the right airline counter and we began the process of weighing ourselves and the bags. I stood on the digital scales and it made a weird clicking sound before the screen cut out automatically.

'Oh shit, I think I've broken it,' I said to the airline employee.

He kind of manoeuvred his head to the side so that he could take the reading and exploded into laughter.

'It is only going to the 105 kilos,' he answered. 'You is more than this.'

I nodded gravely. All I could think was that these planes weren't designed for people of my mass, and that I'd have to refund my ticket and walk all the way back to Jiri. But he waved me over to an ancient looking set of scales, big enough to weigh an elephant on. I felt pretty important for some reason. I weighed in at 106kg, six kilos lighter than I was when I left my home. If you want to lose weight while eating as many Snickers bars as you want, just book a flight to Nepal and go wandering in the high Himalayas for 25 days. That'll do it.

A heated debate broke out between Subash, the airline employees and the airport manager (who happened to be the owner of the lodge I stayed at, who was pouring the largest portions of rum I'd ever seen). It seemed that the 106kg of me, combined with the 16kg of my big backpack and the 10kg of my day pack were way over the personal weight allocation. The airport manager had taken my side and had casually strolled over and stood by Subash. He was now shouting down the airline dudes. I was smiling, in spite of myself. There is something very strange about Nepali people speaking Nepali. They can be so animated that it is easy to work out what they are talking about, even though I understood only one word in the entire conversation. The airport manager was now pointing at Subash and did a he's-a-very-small-man impression, pointed at me and raised two fingers and pointed at the airline ticket he was now holding.

'He is wanting to charge you more monies for the more weight,' Subash turned and told me over his shoulder.

'Yeah I know, they're all the same,' I answered. 'Tell them I am very big, you are very small and I paid for both tickets.'

'Yes, your friend here is a saying that now.'

'Yeah I thought so.'

The airline employee broke into a huge smile, shrugged his shoulders in defeat and then handed Subash two boarding passes.

'You should thank this man, he just saved you a lot of money.'

I did thank him and then headed to security. I really could not work this out. You put your bag on a little table and walked through a metal-detection machine, then got felt up by an incredibly intimate security guard. Maybe I imagined it, but I think he winked at me. Then you grabbed your bag and proceeded into the departure lounge. How did they know what was in my bag? It could have been 10 kilos of C4.

It was only 7am and already the building was crowded with hopeful flyers. There was a fair bit of cloud around, and there was a general consensus that it would be a short day of flying in and out of Lukla. 7.30am came and went, as did 8.30am. There were no screens to indicate what might be happening and why there weren't any planes coming or going; no screens to tell us why our flight was now an hour and a half late. Eventually a man sitting next to us, a resident of Kathmandu, placed a call, presumably to Kathmandu airport, and was informed that flights out of Kathmandu were delayed due to bad weather at their end. Subash eavesdropped on the conversation and began relaying the gossip.

It didn't really bother me. They say few people remain unchanged after trekking for a long period of time in the Himalayas. Some people find a sense of spirituality that they did not have before, other people become more confident in their own abilities, some people talk more, some people talk less, but I found myself to be entirely unchanged bar one little thing. I can now sit in a room and just *do nothing*. I am fantastic at it. I can sit and stare at a wall, not even necessarily watching paint dry, but just a plain old wall and be quite content. Does that make me a better person than I was before I came to this Himalayan Kingdom? Well, I suppose it does.

Throw into the room a bunch of people to stare at, and I found myself to be quite happy that the plane was delayed. I didn't have to be anywhere, do anything, or walk anywhere. So I just sat there with a look of contentment sprawled across my bearded face. Sometimes I stared out at the beautiful, nameless peak dominating the view across the airfield, glistening in the morning sunshine. Sometimes I moved my right leg, which was resting at a 90-degree angle on my left leg, and introduced a role reversal with the resting leg becoming the supporter. It was all very Zen.

With the time fast approaching 9am, there was a sudden hive of activity. Security guards began pouring out onto the tarmac and porters began frantically trying to do their best headless chicken impressions, running around with baggage trolleys and hurtling them into each other as they jostled for the best position to load the incoming plane. Everyone stood up and craned their necks to see which airline was going to be the first to arrive.

'If this our plane, our airlines, then we must be quick,' Said Subash with great determination in his voice.

'I thought we were on the first flight no matter what.'

He rolled his eyes at me, gave me a *what-the-hell-would-you-know* look and basically told me that this was not Australia, this was Nepal, and that I should do exactly what he tells me to do. A plane came roaring up the runway and did a quick U-turn in front of the terminal before the pilot cut the engines. It was our airline. Subash shot up, leap-frogged about nine people and all of a sudden was the first person in the queue. He looked around and saw that I was about 20 metres behind him and about 10th in the queue, and rolled his eyes at me again before turning his focus to being the first one on that plane. I felt like giving him the finger but I showed a great deal of restraint. Perhaps I had changed.

The incoming passengers streamed out, many looking a little over-weight and slightly daunted by the look of trim, tanned and bearded outbound trekkers. The pilot and co-pilot got out for a smoke. They were dressed in black leather pilot outfits from the 80s and had proud, exaggerated moustaches. Subash motioned furiously that I should join at the front of the queue, which I did this time, apologising all the way to everyone I passed. I made an *I'm-sorry-but-my-guide-made-me-do-*

it kind of face and eventually boarded the plane in second place. We sat right at the front of this poxy little plane that would not have been out of place in a museum, buckled up and sat with nervous anticipation.

I pulled my camera out, flicked it onto HD recording mode and began to record the event. Then I thought: *No, I'd rather enjoy this moment*, switched the camera off and looked out the window as the pilots kicked the engines back to life and commenced their pre-flight checks.

All too soon we were off. There was no conventional pause at the top of the runway to commence final checks - these guys meant business – and within seconds we had reached the top of the strip and commenced a gut-wrenching drop as the engines began to do their thing. You know that feeling you get when a roller coaster begins a downward spiral, or that feeling in the stomach when a car goes down a dip in the road too fast, or that feeling when you begin to accelerate in free-fall from bungee jumping or presumably sky-diving? Well that's what you get in your guts when the plane begins its take-off on Lukla airstrip.

The runway is simply that steep. It has to be so you can pick up enough speed to actually *take-off*, instead of plummeting to your death off the side of the mountain. It has to be that steep so that planes landing can slow down in time. Within milliseconds we were at the end of the runway – the pilot used every single millimetre at his disposal – and I'm not going to say we took off. More like we carried on at the same height for a while as the ground dropped steeply away from us. It was all terribly exciting. I could not imagine coming the other way and flying into the face of a mountain.

Eventually the pilots decided to stop pissing around and we began to climb. We were fast approaching a large wall of cloud. I have flown enough in small aircraft, some smaller than this one we were in now, around the top end of Australia's Northern Territory, to know that clouds of that magnitude make big bumps for little flimsy man-made machines that glide through the air. The pilot knew this too, but he inexplicably waited until the last possible second, just as we were about to be utterly enveloped by a mean-looking cloud so large that it could hide Everest several times over, before pulling back hard on the control yoke. The result was another gut-wrenching incident as the plane sharply climbed above the cloud.

Pissed off that we had just avoided it's grasp, the cloud gave us a huge bump anyway and I was made to feel very happy that I had firmly fastened my seatbelt. As I was directly behind the pilots I could see all the instrumentation. I could have flicked the pilot's ear had I so desired, and let's be honest here for a second, he probably deserved it after his little stunt. My eyes became drawn to a little flashing light directly in front of the co-pilot, which intermittently read 'Terrain Warning'. You could fly just metres over peaks in this cloud and have absolutely no idea. I'd sat on the wrong side of the plane, as Subash's side afforded beautiful views of the Himalayas, while my side seemed to be mostly dusty hills. A few weeks ago I called those hills *mountains*, but perhaps Subash was right all along. I had scoffed at his notion that something with a pointy top that was greater in elevation than 4000m could be considered a hill, yet these rises surrounding the Lamjura Pass looked like little children compared with the giants we had been wandering between but a few days ago.

Clouds swirled around the highest places and we began to enter the Kathmandu Valley. Here, dust reigned supreme. Soon, everything disappeared from sight and we could see nothing but a gathering brown haze. I lost interest with looking out the window, but instead became fixated on a dial that was going round and round in an anti-clockwise direction.

It told me we were at 5900 feet. I did a very rough conversion, realised we were at about 1800 metres, recalled that Kathmandu was between 1300m and 1400m, and then by process of deduction realised we were but a few hundred metres from the ground. I looked out the window again and strained my eyes, willing them to pierce the brown smog, but they saw nothing.

I turned my attention once again to the dial, which had us fast approaching 5000ft. I watched as it flicked past that milestone, before looking out the window once more. Just as I did, I caught fleeting glimpses of houses and five-to-six storey buildings rising out of the gloom. Within seconds we had cleared them and were now gliding over a large field made up of dead grass. Then we hovered just inches above a bumpy bitumen runway, before touching down hard on the beautiful black top. I high-fived myself inside my own head, before thinking: *Well, it's a real shit kinda day in Kathmandu.* We bumped our way along an airstrip desperately in need of an over-lay. I should know.

We piled out of the plane and I bumped my head for one final time in Nepal. I smiled at the air hostess who had essentially the easiest, but maybe the scariest job in the entire world.

All she did was bring us one tiny piece of candy about half way through the flight. She said the words, 'Mind your head, sir,' a millisecond too late. It reminded me of all the beautiful places I had been to, and as it didn't hurt, it told me I'd finally killed about every single nerve my forehead had to offer. That may just come in handy in rugby matches in years to come.

A mini bus pulled up and we dutifully boarded it before being made to sit there for 25 minutes while one poor bloke unloaded all the luggage into a cart, dragged it over to the minibus and attached it to some sort of tow bar at the back. I really wanted to go and give him a hand but we were locked in this bus with no way out and the driver had disappeared. It was probably not a good idea anyway. He probably would have dropped dead on the spot if a white man had offered to give him some help.

Chapter Nineteen

FROM TREKKER TO TOURIST

Collecting our baggage was of course fun. I watched as humans became animals right in front of my very eyes. There was literally 12 people on that plane and so we literally had to collect 12 bags, yet everyone wanted their bags first. In Nima's absence, Subash had assumed the role of porter-guide and he was going nuts at the makeshift rack-cum-baggage carousel. It was most entertaining watching it from the back of the crowd, but heaven forbid you got caught up in that madness. I laughed out loud as a Nepali woman, perhaps 50 years old, pushed a young German man out of her way as he approached his backpack. He looked like he was about to burst into tears.

The funniest thing about the entire ordeal was, that if these people had formed an orderly queue, even the last person in that queue would have received their bag about 19 times faster than the first person did when they were behaving like puppies fighting over their mother's milk.

We found a taxi driver, or rather he found us. He was a friendly chap, chatting away to Subash about our trip over the past month or so. Of course I knew this as Subash was listing in chronological order the towns we'd visited along the way, not because I had suddenly learnt Nepali. I was far more likely to die in this taxi than I was in that plane, but suddenly the utter chaos of Kathmandu's roads felt rather safe. I found myself smiling as we narrowly avoided a cow, and bursting into a small but controlled bout of laughter as the driver narrowly avoided another taxi that was reversing down the middle lane of a three-lane highway. Apart from the pollution pouring in through the open windows, this was living!

We pulled up at Hotel Friend's Home. When I had managed to secure some form of internet in Namche Bazaar a few days earlier, I had trawled the internet for a vacancy at this hotel, but I never managed to actually secure a booking. Subash had assured me they would find a room for me because I had been a guest there before.

'Yes, but Subash, how can they find a room for me if they don't actually have any rooms available?' I'd asked him, a little confused.

'No problems man,' he'd countered. 'You is staying there before, so they is finding you the rooms. If not, you can stay at Hotel Mum's Home.'

'You just made that name up right then didn't you?'

'What you is meaning?'

'I mean, is Hotel Mum's Home a real place, or did you just make that up?'

'Is a real, man! Is owned by the same peoples as the friend's home.'

'You should tell them it is a ridiculous name!' I said, while flicking the ridiculous name into a Google search, dubious that anything would come up. I should have known. It was legit. 'You do realise, Subash, that people go on holiday to crazy places like Kathmandu because they don't want the comfort of their mother's home. If you want something like that you go somewhere like Paris or Rome or New York. Not Kathmandu.'

'It not my hotel,' he replied, immediately absolving himself from the argument. I didn't blame him really. 'What you is meaning Kathmandu is the crazy places?'

'I *is* meaning that any city that has the cows running down main streets in the middle of the city is a crazy places,' I answered. He'd kind of made a weird shaking motion with his head, as if this were the most normal thing in the world.

Back in the present, we walked through the doors of the hotel, and the little man that had served me tea and breakfast in the morning almost exploded out of his skin with excitement to see me return to the hotel. It was as though I'd just offered him a million dollars. He covered the distance between me and him in about two seconds flat, so fast he resembled a defender in a game of rugby and for a second I thought I was about to get tackled. Instead he paused just short, held out his hand and beamed a most terrific smile at me. *What have I done to deserve this?* His English was limited, so he checked himself, nodded his head deliberately and said, 'Sir! How you, sir? How trekking, sir?'

I found myself wanting to tell him all about it, but instead I replied, 'I am very good. Trekking very good. You have a beautiful country, my friend.'

'Thank you, sir. Thank you,' he beamed a smile at me that almost melted my heart.

I took my leave and walked up to reception where Subash had been putting forward my case. The receptionist, the same man that had checked me in when I'd first arrived at this hotel, turned and offered me a smile that I will remember until I'm old and grey. He was bubbling with excitement to see me return.

'Hey, he's back!' I heard a voice call from behind me. It was the manager of the trekking agency. 'How was everything my friend?'

'Everything was great, thank you!' I answered. I was beginning to feel a bit like a celebrity. Even the few tourists in the lobby were giving me looks like: *Who is this famous guy? I do recognise him from somewhere....*

'How was the guide?'

'I think you gave me the best guide and porter in all of Nepal,' I answered.

'Very good, very good,' he said, while stepping forward and giving me an affectionate

289

tap on the shoulder. 'Please come and take tea with me at our agency.'

'Yeah I will, tomorrow. I just want to relax today.'

'Excuse me, sir,' a different voice called from behind me. 'Of course we is having the room for you, sir,' the receptionist said once more. 'It will be ready in just 10 minutes, sir, so please drink the tea with us.'

I looked at Subash, who had his arms folded, and the smuggest looking I-told-you-so expression sprawled across his face. I went back to the first man and he offered me tea while I sat with Subash in the lobby. I arranged to meet him at midday so that he could show me where his agency was. I wanted to arrange some tours to various places around Kathmandu the following day, and as I didn't have a phone I did not really know how to get in contact with him. Barely two minutes later, a set of keys dangled down over my shoulder and I looked up to see my receptionist mate with another big smile spread from ear to ear. I took the keys and took my leave of Subash. I had things to do. I had a big-ass pile of trekker sweat and grime to rid myself of. It was going to be glorious!

*

The room was small but decorated with the same dark-stained-wood-on-a-cream-background feel that I had experienced with the other room, which lent a soothing, elegant touch. The bed was ginormous and after my shower I could not wait to jump on it. It was about the most comfortable thing in Nepal, that bed, after some of the places I'd tried to sleep at. Within seconds I could feel myself dozing off to sleep. It took great willpower to snap myself out of it, sit up, grab the remote and switch the TV on, but I did it. I flicked through dozens of local channels and others beamed in from India, 99% of which were utterly shite, the other 1% just good enough for a ten-second watch to laugh at the appalling acting.

It was a different animal, television in this part of the world. In Hollywood movies (some of them), the actors and actresses are so fantastically good at acting that it makes them seem like they are not acting at all – that they are in fact just relaying real-life events to you through the big screen. In Bollywood and whatever television or movie industry they have in Nepal, it is the polar opposite. They are so exaggerated and abnormal in their portrayal of characters so as not to seem real, and hence they differentiate between real-life and acting. It was dreadful really. The actors and actresses had about as much acting talent as a pubic hair. They were crap.

I was relieved when I stumbled upon an English speaking movie channel, but it was an Adam Sandler movie, and he tried his absolute best to disprove my earlier comments that Hollywood actors could act, so I was forced into more flicking. Luckily I came across the ever-reliable BBC World, which is good watching for about an hour until they press the replay button and you are subject to the same 'news' over and over again, all day. Luckily, however, the ever unreliable Kathmandu electricity was to intervene and a power cut made up my mind for me. *Should have turned that rubbish off anyway.* I dressed and planned to do a lap of Thamel before meeting Subash back at the hotel.

*

Subash found me sitting in the lobby drinking yet another cup of bloody tea. Unfortunately, I'd only just taken the first sip as he walked in the door.

'Wow, look at you!' I exclaimed. My trekking guide had entered wearing black designer jeans and an almost skin-tight grey designer top with a Ralph Lauren logo on it (I say that because it couldn't have been real, but it was a bloody good try). He had a large, green and almost awkward feminine bracelet attached to his wrist and his hair was as well-groomed and puffed up as I'd ever seen it. He kind of stood there in the doorway expecting me to jump up and follow him, because that is what I did; but a cup of tea could not be taken too lightly in a country obsessed by it, so I waved him in and motioned to the little kitchen attendant that he should get Subash a cup as well. We sat in silence for a while, I think mostly because we were enjoying the comfort of the leather couches too much for words.

Within a few minutes we were finished and I followed as Subash took me on a tour of the back streets. They were mercifully void of cars so an act as simple as walking down the street suddenly became safe again. We were walking parallel to one of the main roads and I could hear the chaos, even if I could not see it. A security guard watched us approach, almost suspiciously, but was immediately defused after hearing a white man salute him in his mother-tongue. He broke into a smile and replied to my greeting.

An old lady wandered out of an old, crumbling building with a small bucket of water in her hand and was about to launch it over the road in combat of the dust. I kind of made a wimpy squealing noise because I realised she hadn't seen me and so I was about to get drenched in filthy water. Despite her age there was absolutely nothing wrong with her hearing. She checked her throw, kind of scowled at me a little bit for being such a drama-queen and waited until I was out of soaking range before expertly spreading that water over the maximum area that could be wetted down by that volume. I feared I would be the talking point while she shared dinner with her family that night and so I vowed not to return the way I had come (it hardly seemed like something I should worry about as I was utterly lost).

A large sign stuck out over the road read: 'Outdoor Himalayan Treks', and it suddenly struck me that 'outdoor' was such a pointless word in the company name. Of course they were outdoor. It would be a bit silly if they were 'Indoor Himalayan Treks'. I don't know why this thought hadn't crossed my mind in the duration of the entire trek, but perhaps it was because I had never actually *been* to this agency before. My mind began to wander, as it sometimes has a tendency of doing, and I had great visions of clients walking on treadmills in large air-conditioned rooms with those large virtual reality head-sets on, showing magnificent 3D footage of the Himalayan mountains.

Ridiculous, I know. Or I could be on to something huge.

Below the sign was the company slogan, and it was an absolute peach. The sign read: 'Outdoor Himalayan Treks: Your no more lonely on this planet!'. Enough said.

The boss had seen me enter and I heard him shout something through an open doorway, and within two-hundredths of a second a boy sprinted out and shot off down the stairs. He returned seconds later with a tray upon which sat three glasses of steaming, milky tea.

'This the same tea like at the bus station,' Subash informed me.

'Ah yes, my favourite!'

'You is a liking the Nepali tea?' Asked the boss, perhaps with a touch of surprise in his voice.

'Yeah I love it,' I replied and took an eager sip from the glass. My taste buds were immediately slapped by a combination of cardamom and cinnamon, and I made a sound like 'Mmmmmmm'. I know that cardamom can be an acquired taste, but I acquired a taste for it long ago and I vowed to have a go brewing this delicious tea when I returned home.

'Subash is telling me that you is wanting to make the tour of the Kathmandu,' said the boss, and I could tell that he was about to enter entrepreneur mode. 'You is having the five days here in Kathmandu. I suggest you fly to Pokhara, see the lake, stay a few nights and even view a little the Annapurna range.'

'Ah mate I appreciate the advice, but I am pretty tired and I don't really want to see Pokhara on this trip. I want to see it, and the Annapurna's too, but I would like to do it properly one day, like I did for the Everest trek.'

As I was talking he had casually strolled over to the far side of the room and was now holding up a cheap billboard clumsily advertising Pokhara. It had a gorgeous picture of the lake, but in the foreground there were these white people from the 80s sporting the fakest smiles I ever had the displeasure of seeing. They were clearly Yanks. When I finished talking, he nodded slowly, clearly wishing he could extract a few more dollars from me. He was a nice man, don't get me wrong, but he was a business man first and foremost.

He put down the billboard, wandered back to his desk, sat down, raised his arms in the air and asked, 'What you want to do then?'

'I don't know mate. No trekking,' I replied, and both he and Subash went into hysterics.

'Ok, ok, no trekking. You tell me.'

'You tell me mate, what do most of the tourists go and see. I want to get a bit of culture from the Kathmandu valley.'

'Ok we can take you to the Changu Narayan. This the famous pilgrimage places. Maybe the Pashupatinath Temple and the Monkey Temple and also the Swayambhu and Baudhanath.'

'Yes, what you just said. All those things.'

'Ok these things, and maybe you go to Nagarkot and is watching the sunsets on the valley?'

'Yep, that too. Sounds good.'

'Ok so you is needing the tour guide.'

'I already have a guide,' I answered, a little confused. I motioned to Subash, who dropped his head in embarrassment.

'My friend, Subash is being the trekking guide, not the touring guide.'

'What's the difference?'

'Here in Nepal we is having the two types. A trekking guides and the touring guides. One can do the city tours and one can do the mountain tours, but they cannot do both. It is so that everybody is getting the monies.'

'Ah I see. Can he still come with me to show me the places?'

'Yes he can, but maybe he is having to walk behind you or in front of you.'

I started laughing, thinking they were joking, but as they showed no signs of joining in I knew they were being serious.

'Also, Subash is the trekking guides, so he is not knowing the thing about these places. You know like the culture and the histories and the things.'

'Yeah that's ok, I will just Google it later.'

'Ok so you is needing the private car for two days. It will take the two days to see these things.'

'Ok,' I answered, but it did sound expensive. The boss got out his calculator and started punching in 17,000 digits, before flipping the calculator around 180 degrees so I could read the damage. It was 10,000 rupees, or US $100, for a car and driver for two full days. You can't really argue with that, so I smiled and shook the man's hand.

'One more thing,' he decided to add. 'I will not pay Subash for this things because he is not a guide. You can pay him whatever you think is fair.'

'No worries, mate,' I answered quickly, because I was going to do that anyway. I arranged to meet them back at the agency the next morning and excitedly hit the supermarket. I bought enough dry noodles to feed greater Kathmandu, some Cadbury's Fruit and Nut bars and a few bottles of juice. Party in *my* room. Woo!

*

I didn't know a great deal about anything much after my head hit the pillow that night. I was, as they say, out like a light, which was not switched back on for another 12 hours. A noise – a painfully familiar noise, annoyingly designed specifically for the task of dragging you away from sleep – was making its presence felt about a foot away from my head. My alarm was going off. I swatted at it absentmindedly for a few seconds before coming to the realisation that this never actually worked. With a sigh that could have killed a flower, I raised my head and pressed the snooze button; but just as I did I remembered that I hadn't given myself any snoozing time as I wanted the longest possible sleep. *Damn you Gordon. Damn you!*

I looked around the room and saw half a dozen empty packets of noodles with their accompanying flavour sachets scattered carelessly on almost every conceivable surface. A guava juice box was on the floor while I was sleeping next to an empty Cadbury chocolate wrapper. *Must have been a good night,* I thought while pushing myself off the bed and into another glorious, hot shower. I could not believe I hadn't scheduled another rest day. What was wrong with my brain? Tip-toeing over the noodle packets, I dressed and made my way down for breakfast. I'm not ashamed to admit that I stopped and stared at a pack of five sitting there on the desk, contemplating whether or not to skip breakfast and just dive back into the dried noodles. Common sense prevailed and I went down the stairs, which told me that both my knees were absolutely screwed. I winced in pain with every step, but by the time I was at the bottom they were beginning to warm up and I was moving with a lot more freedom.

'Good morning, sir,' my little friend greeted me with a smile so big I thought it was going to tear his face into two different bits.

'Good morning, how are you?'

'Fine, sir,' he answered. He was always fine.

300

'Milk tea, two pieces of toast and two fried eggs, sir?' he asked, but he already knew the answer. I ordered the same thing every morning.

'Yes, thank you very much,' I replied, while I got sucked into the buffet. I was fuelled up and ready to do battle with the monkeys at the temple. I had visited the monkey temple in Ubud, Bali, some years before and the monkeys had taken a serious disliking to me. We reckoned this was because I was probably the hairiest human being the monkeys had ever seen, and they had mistaken me for a large Rwandan mountain gorilla that had come to assert my authority over the dominant males. They screeched at me, one attacked my shoe, yet they didn't bat a monkey eye lid at any other person there. I would just beat my chest, cry out *hoo hooooo haaa haaa* and they would run away with their tales between their legs, and I'd acquire some new territory in the process with full mating rights.

I brushed my teeth, sent a sausage to the sea-side (or wherever they go in Nepal) and eagerly stepped onto the street. From trekker to tourist. I was well rested, full of fish and noodles, only at 1300m above sea level and feeling like two million bucks.

I found Subash at the agency, but we didn't have long, so he ushered me out the door and back onto the street where we'd wait for our driver. I'd opted to have a car without air-conditioning as I wanted to have my window down and drink in the Kathmandu buzz, the vibe, the atmosphere. But all I ended up drinking in was a shit-load of dust and exhaust fumes. The car had pulled up at 9am sharp and was driven by a loveable looking fat man with the face of a small child, but by 9.05am I was deeply regretting my decision. A couple of extra bucks and I could have been soaking it all up in beautiful, artificially filtered air. You live and you learn. Well, not in my case, but some people do.

We negotiated the maze of Kathmandu, at one point making five left turns in succession, giving me the impression that we were, in fact, lost and going around in circles. Eventually we shot up a hill and then confronted a carpark teaming with taxis and mini busses. We were at the monkey temple.

Also known as Swayambhunath, the Monkey Temple lies on top of a hill on the western side of Kathmandu. The name the Tibetans have for the temple is translated as 'sublime trees', and it was easy to see why. Enormous trees graced us with an abundance of shade, while a multitude of prayer flags strung from giant to giant flapped contentedly in the breeze. There was little dust up here and I could hear beautiful Buddhist chanting drifting on the wind down from a higher place. I took a deep breath, paid my entrance fee and stepped into this most peaceful of places. A crowd had gathered in a circular pattern ahead of us and so we approached to see what all the fuss was about. People were throwing coins into little buckets that made up a strange statue.

'This is bringing the good lucks,' Subash informed me.

'We need to have a go at this,' I replied, but I didn't have any coins.

However, there was a man there whose job it was to change people's notes to coins for a small commission. I spent about three bucks on coins, and soon Subash and I were pitting out skills against each other in fierce competition. Nepal vs. Australia. Final score: Nepal 7 – 8 Australia. It was an important away victory for the men in gold. I led a deflated Subash up a large set of stairs that we barely noticed past a group of monkeys that barely even acknowledged our existence. This had a far holier feel to it than the temple in Bali. At the top sat a large domed stupa with a golden turret on top that had yet more prayer flags strung from the tip to the surrounding temple buildings.

All around the area were little shops selling Buddhist memorabilia and cheap trinket-y tourist crap. It was a little tacky. We did a loop of the stupa, spinning the prayer wheels as we went and absorbed the mesmerising smells of burning incense, and stopped to watch a monkey or two strut their stuff before descending the stairs once more to find our driver. I'm not going to say I rushed it, but despite the history of the place – the site has been a religious landmark for some 1500 years – it was really just a round concrete dome with a set of eyes painted on top of it. I felt the spirituality of the place. I get it. But 20 minutes of shoeing away hopeful merchants whilst keeping a watchful eye out for cheeky monkeys was quite enough.

Soon we were whizzing through the streets once more, off to see Boudhanath, a World Heritage Site, which was essentially just another stupa, only bigger. Instead of paraphrasing someone else, I shall quote the Boudhanath Area Development Committee's brochure, which was given to me upon paying a modest entrance fee:

'The Great Stupa of Boudhanath stands approximately 6km north-east from centre of

Kathmandu valley. Surrounded by hills, Boudhanath stupa is a jewel point in the centre of a natural mandala, a store of sacred energy. It is one of the most important place of pilgrimage for the Buddhist.'

We walked down a wide alleyway before a giant stupa appeared right in front of us. This was more like it.

It was surrounded by buildings of typically ancient Kathmandu architecture, some of which were decorated in the brightest of colours. All the colours of the prayer flag. You thought I was going to say rainbow, didn't ya? We wandered around, myself in awe of this gargantuan structure. Pilgrims from all over the world had dispersed themselves randomly around the place. Some prayed. Some sat in silent contemplation, others meditated. We did a complete circuit of the stupa, taking about ten minutes, before deciding to go up close. The temperature was probably in the mid-twenties, but there was no breeze here.

We wandered around further until we came across a Buddhist monk, a little below us, who looked to be setting up a couple of musical instruments. We stopped and waited. After a few moments he began to beat a drum with one hand while playing a stringed instrument with the other, and then began to chant in a crystal clear voice, clearer than a beautiful blue sky on a Himalayan morning. As if on cue, as though he had summoned it himself, the wind suddenly picked up and gently caressed the prayer flags hanging above our heads. A shiver went down my spine and I sat down in awe, having experienced the most spiritual moment of my entire life. I could have sat there forever, in that moment, and been content, but all too soon the monk had finished his chanting and began to pack up his things. He looked up, made brief eye contact with me and we both nodded a silent understanding of what had just happened before he turned his back and walked into the temple.

I mouthed a 'Wow!' to Subash, unable to speak, before getting up and continuing on our way.

'That was awesome!' I said after a while.

'Yes, this is the chanting things,' he replied, a little underwhelmed.

'Did you see that wind? It was calm and then just started immediately when he began chanting.'

'It was a feeling like a this,' he replied again, this time with a smile creeping across his face. He was happy that I had felt it too.

'All this spirituality has made me hungry, you want some lunch?'

'Yes man, I didn't have the breakfasts until now.'

'Ok man, where is a good place?'

'I don't know. You is asking me in the mountains and I am telling you the very best of places, but I don't know here. I think every place is good.'

I gave him a dubious look and he laughed.

'Ok let's look!' he said and we wandered some more, this time our eyes turned away from the stupa and towards to the many restaurants. Most were three or four storey buildings, and most had lovely-looking rooftop terraces that afforded elevated views of the stupa. We came across a Bhutanese restaurant that we were about to continue walking past.

'You know, I have never had Bhutanese food before. You?' I enquired.

'Never man.'

'Ok, first time for everything,' I said, and then ushered Subash inside to find out if they were open.

They were open, but we were the only guests, which is never a good sign, but we nonetheless pushed on up the stairs until we found the rooftop and took a well-earned seat. The breeze that the monk had conjured was in full flow up here, and we kicked back and ordered a couple of beers and just relaxed. It suddenly felt like I was on holiday.

I looked at the menu while sipping on my Carlsberg (they didn't have Everest Beer or a Bhutanese beer), but was a little perplexed as to what to order. I didn't recognise the name of a single dish.

When the waiter returned I asked Subash to translate for me.

'What is your favourite Bhutanese food?' I asked the man.

'He is saying that it is all good.'

'If he was having lunch with us now, what would he order?'

'He said he would have the Bhutan platter.'

'And what is that?'

'He said it was a collection of the things. Like some of the soups, a curries and the things like this. But he is telling me it is very hot food, maybe it is a too hot for you.'

'I'll have that then, exactly how he would have it,' I decided without hesitation. 'What will you have Subash?'

He looked a little sheepish before choosing the cheapest thing on the menu. I saw what he was pointing to.

'Do you really want that? Aren't you hungry?'

'Yes am hungry man, but this is expensive things.'

'Come on, this is the first time we are trying the Bhutanese food, don't you want the platter?'

'You pay too much to me already man,' he said, but would not hold my eye.

'Subash it's no problem man, you deserve it. Please. Have the platter.'

I looked at the waiter and held up two fingers. Subash smiled in defeat and was happy again. The platter cost US $5.

Before long the waiter brought back a big steaming bowl of rice and four accompanying dishes. Two were interesting cheesy soups that were very spicy indeed. The other two were delicious chicken curries. One of the cheese dishes was the Ema Datshi, and it is to Bhutan what Dal Bhat is to Nepal. It is the national dish, made with a mix of chillies and the local cheese of Datshi. I'm going to say I enjoyed it a lot, but it wouldn't actually be something I'd eat on a regular basis. Cheesy curry soup is a step I'm just not ready to take yet, but I'm very happy we tried something new. The chicken curry was magnificent, and hot enough to knock your socks off. I was in heaven. I looked over at Subash and he wasn't in heaven. Sweat was pouring from his brow and he was struggling his way through the soups.

'Are you ok?' I asked.

'Yes, ok man.'

'You don't look ok.'

'Yes, ok, but very much it is too spicy for me.'

'I can tell.'

'It is the very nice foods, but too hot for Nepali peoples.'

The waiter brought out some complementary desserts for us, which looked like a big white slop, but was very sweet and tasty. Subash launched his soup to the side and began coating his tongue gratefully with the white slop. I could do nothing but laugh.

About half an hour later we were hurtling down a bumpy road, me banging my head on that handle above me for the 32nd time, before firing up a hill to visit another temple. I was a bit over it, if I'm honest. We pulled up to some big steel gates and the driver sat on his horn for a good ten seconds until a security guard came rushing out and begged him to shut the hell up. Subash turned around to face me in the back and said, 'This place is closed today for the monk's meditation lessons.'

'Whoops, they wouldn't have enjoyed that noise he just made.'

'No, they is a very angry.'

'Should we go?'

'Yes, better we go.'

The driver pulled around the corner out of sight of the security guard. Then Subash uttered something and the driver pulled the car over.

'You would like to walk down this hills and meet the driver at the bottom?' He asked me.

'Ok, I like downhill,' I replied, and the driver erupted into hysterical laughter. It was probably the first thing he'd understood from me and was delighted.

It was a pleasant stroll. Being higher up than the valley floor we were treated to an excellent view of the sprawl that is Kathmandu. We were far enough away from the mayhem that it was actually quite clear and dust free, and we were treated to excellent views back up the way to the temple, which I have to admit was very impressive. After 10 minutes or so we found the fat driver standing outside of the car doing battle with half a dozen school children all dressed up in shirts and ties, trying to bash him playfully with some branches they had ripped from a nearby tree. The poor bloke was running around theatrically, trying to get himself in between the children and his car to protect it. Each time the children tapped the car they would go into hysterics, literally rolling around on the ground with laughter.

'Why have they got those branches?' I asked Subash while joining in on the laughter.

'They is going down the hills and stealing it from the farmer down there. It is having the little fruits on it they is liking to eat.'

'Won't they get in trouble?'

'They is the children. They can do anything they want.'

One of the boys suddenly took an interest in the camera I had around my neck.

'Mister, mister!' he called out at the top of his voice. 'Pleased taking me the photograph!'

'Yes, yes the photograph!' the rest of the children called out in unison.

'Ok, ok, sit on the wall,' I answered, and they scurried in as quickly as they could, suddenly the best behaved children in the world.

'Ok, ready, one...,' I began a countdown, but it was the children that finished it off, with a choir of little voices chanting, 'two, three!'

They entered a state of jubilation and I took a few photos of them.

'Come here, come here,' I ushered them over to show them their pictures on my little play-back screen. They were elated, and made me zoom in on all of them one-by-one. After they'd seen themselves they took off and began running around in circles, surely the happiest children on the face of the planet. I thought about what kind of world the children in Australia and other rich countries grew up in, with their iPads and games and apps and X-boxes, and wondered if their computer games ever made them as happy as a single photograph had made these little guys, or as happy as these kids were playing games with a friendly-looking stranger and his car.

The little boy, (the menace and the instigator) took a step away from me, looked me square in the eye and said, 'Mister, thank you for my photograph!'

'You're welcome,' I answered and watched as he was overcome by a fit of laughter, and broke into a run with both arms outstretched like an aeroplane. *I wonder if they're always like this, or there is something in that fruit.*

We piled into the car and began driving off. I turned and looked out the rear window to see us being chased by the children and their branches as they launched one final assault on the car. When it was beyond their grasp, they jumped up and down with their little arms around each other.

*

We were now on our way to see Pashupatinath, a holy place on the Bagmati River, revered by both Hindus and Buddhists alike, but probably most widely known by visitors to Kathmandu as the cremation site for Hindus.

The driver dropped us at about a 10-minute walk from the main entrance and we were forced to walk down a narrow street, lined with a thousand shops that sold exactly the same merchandise. It was mostly items of a religious nature, statues, bracelets and necklaces; but no one was buying anything. It did make me wonder how on earth these people survived with their little shops as their only livelihoods. I supposed that business would boom during days of special spiritual significance, but that was only an assumption. As we neared the entrance, a shifty looking man clocked us, immediately matched our walking pace and began to hassle Subash. They talked for a few minutes, before he turned his attention to me, asking, 'My friend, you is wanting the guide for the Pashupatinath temple?'

'No thanks man, I am just looking today.'

'But you is needing to know the histories and the things like this and I am the very good guide.'

'Nah you're ok,' I answered again, this time deliberately quickening my pace. He again sped up, and continued hassling me. On my travels throughout the world, I have become accustomed to people trying to hustle, but this man was something else. He got angry.

He began to shout at Subash in Nepali.

'Hey mate, I don't want a bloody guide, alright?' I said, raising my voice a little.

'This man is the trekking guides. He cannot be the city guides. He is stealing from my businesses!'

'That man is my friend. He is not my guide. Now piss off!'

He looked as though he was going to shout something else at us, but instead checked himself, turned on his heal and stormed off.

'What a wanker!' I said to Subash.

'Yes, is,' he replied and then we quickly left the scene before any more unwanted attention was thrown our way. I paid an enormous entrance fee (something like US $10, which is very expensive in Nepali terms. The Buddhist temples only charged a dollar or two) and stepped into a large open courtyard. A group of five people sat over to our left, dressed in brightly coloured garments of orange and green. In front of them was an ancient-looking amp with a microphone attached. A couple of Indian-sounding instruments began to be played by a few members of the group before the man with the mic began singing softly. It was a traditional Nepali song, but his voice was dry and scratchy and it made me cringe a little bit.

'These are the blind singers,' Subash whispered.

'Really? All of them?'

'Yes, all.'

Good on them, I thought. But it didn't change the fact that they were atrocious musicians. I dropped a couple of dollars into the basket, hoping the lead singer would spend it on singing lessons, before walking a bit further into the temple. There were a few cows (the sacred animal in the Hindu religion) scattered around the area and they just looked so out of place. Thousands of pigeons flocked the courtyard floor, but would get spooked occasionally and take to the sky.

'Wish we had an umbrella,' I called to Subash as it began to rain shit around us. He laughed and grabbed my arm as we jogged a little further down and away from the shit storm. We approached a large archway, but a sign placed directly out front informed us that only Hindus were permitted past this point.

'Doesn't seem fair,' I said.

'No problems man, shall we go and see the funerals?'

'Yeah ok.'

We headed back the way we had come and back out the main gate where the guide was waiting, still fuming. He began to follow us as we headed towards the *ghats.* Then the bastard waited until we were walking past a security guard before erupting into another shouting match with Subash. Fortunately, we had outsmarted him. As he joined us I noticed he was watching Subash intently, so I dropped back a good 50 feet and went to a little stall and bought a drink of water. I could hear him shout the words 'trekking guide'. The security guard looked around and shrugged, as if to say: *Then where the hell is his client?* I waited until Subash was well and truly inside and out of our line of vision, before I casually began to follow him. I walked past the security guard, but he shouted for me to stop. I turned slowly, thinking we had been busted.

I turned to find the man with the biggest, friendliest grin sprawled across his face.

'My friend, ticket? Ticket?' he asked.

'Yes ticket having,' I answered him with a smile to match. We were best of mates and I hoped that bastard guide could see that. I showed him my ticket and he bowed ever so slightly before putting out an open hand, allowing me to pass.

I found Subash on the bridge that connected the two banks and we kind of raised our eyebrows and rolled our eyes at each other. I looked around and took in the scene. A string of six or seven ghats lined just one side of the river, which was really just a small trickle of water. Monkeys shrieked and played in the river, splashing water and chasing birds. One of the ghats was ablaze in a roaring fire, which made the air thick with smoke. On the other side of the bank sat dozens of onlookers, coming to witness the cremation ceremony. A pair of boys were knee-deep in the river a little further down, and were collecting bits of bamboo and timber that were floating down the stream, which they then piled high onto a makeshift trolley that they dragged along the riverbed.

We went and sat with the onlookers, where the mood was nothing short of solemn. I watched as a group of about eight men carried an old woman into sight, before carefully placing her up on the pyre and retreating to say a few words. I took in the whole scene. The person that was already on fire was almost completely cremated, apart from his lower legs and feet, which were sticking out a little from

319

the flames. A man realised, went over and adjusted some tinder so that the flames soon enveloped what was left.

Back at the other ghat the men carried the woman's body around the pyre three times, before placing her back down. They unwrapped the garment which cloaked her entire body from head to toe, revealing her face to me for the first time. "You aren't that old," I said to the woman, before a member of the family lit a small fire in her mouth which quickly encompassed her entire body, and within minutes she couldn't be seen behind the smoke and flames. It was a slightly bizarre and alien thing for me to witness, but I can say quite honestly that I felt nothing inside. Not sadness, not disgust. I can only really say that I felt quite honoured to be able to witness this side of a very different culture to my own. And I'm not being mean here or insensitive or anything like that, but the place smelt like a barbecue. It really did.

'Let's go Subash, I've seen enough.'

As we were walking out of the temple for the last time, two black jeeps pulled up in a hurry, and out jumped almost a dozen men in military attire with semi-automatic machine guns slung over their shoulders. They checked the area as Subash and I stood there dumbfounded. One man, the leader, raised a hand in the direction from which they had come and suddenly a few more cars pulled up. A man, probably about 60 years old, came striding confidently forward with two armed guards on either shoulder.

'Who is he?' I whispered urgently to Subash.

'He is Pushpa Kamal Dahal. The people is calling him Prachanda also.'

'Why is he here?'

Subash called out to the man next to him to make the appropriate enquiries, before telling me, 'His daughter died.'

'Ah shit. Why does he have so much security?'

'Because he is former Prime Minister of Nepal and he is the Mao. You know what this is? Is the communist party and he is the leaders.'

It was an amazingly interesting place. But now, please, let me pass you over to the Pashupati Area Development Trust Council's remarkably persuasive information brochure for some flowery descriptions:

'*No visitor to Kathmandu would like to miss the opportunity to visit the Pashupatinath site, which is so richly endowed with places he would like to see and objects he would love to buy. Here there are temples and idols so esoteric and monumental for the lenses of their cameras. There are shops which sell objects that look mystic and magical. He can pack 'golden' monkeys jumping playfully about into his movie roll.'*

What are you waiting for?

*

It was 3pm by the time I made it back to Friend's Home and mercifully the power was on. I spent the afternoon reading, watching BBC News, listening to music and picking Kathmandu dust boogers out of my nose.

*

The following morning, we had just one more temple to tick off, which was a bit of a relief. They were just getting a bit same-sy. I know I can make it sound like a chore, but it did feel really good to be getting my hands dirty with a bit of culture.

This time it was Changu Narayan, the single oldest monument in Nepal, dating back as far as the third century AD. It was a fair old drive to get there, but lineally it wasn't actually that far from the centre of Kathmandu. If we'd raced a bird it would have left us for dead.

We drove up another hill and we were confronted with a small village of sublimely unique architecture, quite unlike anything I'd seen anywhere else in the world, let alone Nepal. We followed a narrow path up through overhanging buildings comprised of red bricks, which had a multitude of power lines strung between them. The ground floor of these buildings was occupied, without exception, by little shops selling more crap. Ugly statues with gargoyles and heads with fifteen eyes. It was just gross and completely underwhelming.

The monument itself was alright. It certainly felt old, although it was nowhere near as impressive as Durbar Square, which I was to find out the following day. However, it was a very important monument. The story goes that (and take it however you will, I don't want to offend any Hindus out there, but I find it a little farfetched) there once was a farmer who owned a cow that produced a great amount of milk. One day this cow began to graze by the same tree every day. However, rather unfortunately, when the cow came back from grazing, the farmer found that the milk had begun to run very low indeed. After a while, a little disgruntled, he began to stalk the cow from afar, hidden in a few bushes. As the cow stood by the tree, a black boy appeared and began to drink the milk straight from the cow. The farmer was infuriated, and later fetched an axe and began hacking into the tree. However, the tree began to bleed actual human blood, and Lord Vishnu appeared, saying he had been beheaded, which had freed him from earlier sins he had committed, and hence had lifted the curse from him (quite how he did this after a beheading I'm not entirely sure). He told the farmer not to despair, and so he didn't. Instead he built a monument to Lord Vishnu at this very spot where I now stood, and began to worship it over 1700 years ago.

There were a few carvings of Lord Vishnu around the monument, but also of Garuda, a humanoid-like bird that served as Vishnu's carrier. Fun fact: Indonesia's national carrier named their airline after this god of the sky. Yay.

I looked around for a very short while, before getting (understandably) distracted by the cutest little puppy dog hunting a leaf.

'Go on, get it!' I egged him on. 'Don't put up with that shit.'

Subash had arrived on the scene, and almost seemed relieved there was extra entertainment to distract him from architecture. We unanimously decided it was time to leave.

'Ok, now we is walking to the Nagarkot,' Subash surprised me.

'Ah ok, how far is that?'

'Maybe take 3 or 4 hours, but it is depending on a you.'

'That's funny, I could have sworn you said 3 or 4 hours just there, right then.'

'Yes, but you is a good walking man, so maybe takes the 3 hours.'

I started laughing. This had to be a joke, but Subash was deadly serious.

'Wait, wait, wait. Let me get this straight. I hire a car for the whole day, and we have to walk for 3 or 4 hours? And what, he meets us at Nagarkot and brings us home?'

'Yes man!'

'Why can't he drive us there?'

'Because we is going for the sunsets. To be seeing the sunsets over the Kathmandu Valley. If we is a driving there, maybe we be there by lunch time, not the sunsets time.'

'Hmmm I dunno mate. I come from a city renowned for its glorious sunsets over the ocean,' I said, trying to get myself out of this. 'And I thought I said no trekking!'

'This is not a trekking things!' He exclaimed. 'This is the walking things.'

I sighed for the 142nd time on this trip, raised my hands in defeat and nodded.

'Ok, it is past 11am, maybe we should have lunch before we go.'

'Good idea,' he answered and pointed to a restaurant that had conveniently appeared right next to us. We walked in and climbed up the stairs to sit on the rooftop, which afforded fine views of the monument. We ordered some food and kicked back in silence while soaking up a delightful breeze that was now in full flow. I wondered if a monk had summoned it from somewhere unseen.

'Hey man, come see this,' Subash called to me from somewhere behind. I got up, stirred from my trance and went to join him on the far side of the roof-top. He pointed down to a little garden bed, which was teeming with marijuana plants.

'Wow, they are growing them up here?'

'Yes man, is growing. You see this one?' He said while pointing to a brown stem that shot up at least a metre from the ground. 'This one is an old one. They is already picking it and is a smoking. This ones are the babies.'

'Not very subtle, growing it in your restaurant in the dining area. As my old housemaster used to say, 'about as subtle as a brick'.

'This is Nepal man, is a normal things.'

Chapter Twenty

SUMMING UP

The stroll to Nagarkot was as uneventful as it was easy. The following morning, I took in the ancient-looking buildings of Durbar Square and absorbed one last feel of a bustling, over-crowded Kathmandu. I was a bit sad. I knew I had to say goodbye to Subash.

'So Mr Gorong,' he was saying to me while I daydreamed over lunch, instantly snapping me out of it. 'When you is coming back to the Nepal?'

'As soon as I possibly can,' I replied truthfully. 'I wanna go see Kangchenjunga next.'

'Yes, is a very good choices. World's third biggest mountain. Is the beautiful countryside, not too many peoples. Maybe sometimes we is camping also.'

'Yeah it looks beautiful. I don't want to go over 5000 metres again though!' I answered with a shudder.

'You won't have to.'

'And I'll only go with you and the Nima, ok?'

'Of course man.'

'Thanks for everything mate. I could not have done any of that without you. Keep in touch.'

We completed a gangsta handshake, brought it in for a manly hug, turned our backs and went our separate ways.

At the airport I joined a long queue for the flight to Kuala Lumpur, lit up on a typically ancient TV screen. After perhaps 20 minutes, the screen flicked off and returned to a state of blackness. Everyone began murmuring and turning their heads. A second later, the flight reappeared on a different screen, about four desks down. What ensued was a *Jumanji*-like stampede, whereby everyone in the middle and back of the queue trampled towards the front of the new check-in counter. Peeved people who were at the front could only shake their heads, pick up their luggage and wander to the back of the new line. Already being at the back, I probably gained a good six spots.

Half an hour later I was still in the queue, while there was not a single airline employee to be seen. And then *zang!* The screen went black. The queuers braced themselves, urgently scanning from left to right to see where it would reappear. And then, the unthinkable. It showed its ugly face back on the original monitor, four rows back to the left! I gave up. I threw my pack up against the rear wall facing back into the terminal and sat down to watch the chaos unfold.

*

Once in the airplane, departing almost two-hours late, we began the push-back. We completed the obligatory 90-degree turn, but just as we stopped the entire left side of the plane slumped down a good half-metre. We stopped after rocking back and forth for a good few seconds. We waited while they disconnected the plane. The engines fired to life. The plane moved forward just an inch before it began rocking violently from side to side. Eventually the pilot gave up and took his foot off the gas.

Then he had another go, with more engine power this time, which was directly proportionate to the increase in violent rocking of the plane. He gave up.

'Ladies and gentleman, we have been taxied into a big pothole,' the captain said grimly. 'I have radioed for them to come and pull us out. Please enjoy the flight.'

'Let's try to take off first,' I heard a middle-aged American man say a few rows in front of me.

We watched with interest as one little tractor came tearing out, then disappeared as it went under the plane. A few seconds later, the plane began rocking from side to side as it attempted to win the tug of war. This was a bloody Boeing 777 for God's sake. This was ridiculous. The rocking stopped and we hadn't moved. Moments later another tractor came shooting over, disappeared under the plane, hooked on to the first guy, and then they simultaneously managed to pull us from the pothole, but with the accompanying rocking at its strongest.

The passengers began contagiously clapping and cheering, so I joined in. The Yank started, for no reason at all, to chant: 'USA! USA! USA!'

So that sums up Nepal right there. A place where even the apron of an international airport has a pothole big enough to swallow a jumbo jet.

I slipped into a state of utter bliss. The greatest mountains in the world slid past my line of vision, I was walking on a glacier, effortlessly taking a pass, viewing beautiful valleys and knife-edged ridges, laughing with locals, arguing with Israelis, herding some yaks, drinking Kukri rum, playing with puppies, eating delicious aromatic food, making life-long friends. It is my happy place. And I can go there anytime I want.

THE END

If you made it this far, congratulations! If you enjoyed this book, or if you hated it, an honest review on Amazon is greatly appreciated by us wannabe authors. Feel free to get in touch if you have any questions, there are multiple contact options on my website www.gordonalexander.org

Thanks and have a great day! - Gordon

Made in the USA
Middletown, DE
04 February 2017